BRINGING HEAVEN DOWN TO EARTH

Book II

meditations on the wisdom of the Rebbe
Rabbi Menachem Mendel Schneerson

by Tzvi Freeman

Published by Class One Press
info@theRebbe.com

ISBN 978-0-9682408-6-1
Printed in USA

Much of the content of this book appeared in
Be Within, Stay Above by the same author
and has been revised for this edition

By the same author:

Bringing Heaven Down To Earth

The Book of Purpose

Men, Women & Kabala

Heaven Exposed

Black Leather Boxes

Permissions and comments:
info@theRebbe.com

For more of the same:
www.chabad.org
www.theRebbe.com
www.DownOnEarth.com
www.TzviFreeman.com

cover design by Izzy Greenberg
cover art by Chuck Carter

reVision

This book has a life. The first time I wrote it, it was titled *Answers*. That was a small book, just the size to fit in your shirt pocket. I printed 5,000 and the binder spoiled the cover.

That's when I composed meditation number 36 in this edition:

> *Failure is wasted if you return only to the place from where you fell. If your plans fail, think bigger, aim higher.*

So I made a bigger book, *Be Within, Stay Above*. I added many meditations and chapters with introductions. Again, I printed 5,000. They were selling well—but then somehow the books were lost. I still don't know how.

Bouncing back can get kind of weary at times. But in truth, I always felt I had pushed that book out too fast. A good book needs a healthy term of gestation. *Bringing Heaven Down To Earth*, after all, spent some 23 years in its womb.

Now, six years later, I've revised almost everything. I've added many meditations, even whole chapters and some of my more popular essays from chabad.org as introductions. I changed the order of the chapters, so that this book picks up where the last one left off. Most important, I've put each meditation again under a fine microscope, demanding of each phrase that it says just what it is supposed to say, of each word that it carries its own weight. Many did not survive.

Blades of grass condense the morning mist into fine droplets of dew, and I have condensed my teacher's wisdom into this small book. Not all my teacher's wisdom, not even a measurable portion. Less than a droplet is to a valley of that fine mist. But as the dew is of the mist—for from where else could it have come?—so these words are of my teacher's wisdom.

I tried to live the thoughts in this book. For many years, they resonated in my mind. Some gave strength, others maturity, some carried me through times I could not otherwise have endured. Eventually, they found a form fit for ink on paper. Then I polished and refined each word many times as best I could.

They are not poems for the lips. They are not pretty ideas for intellectual games. They are not necessarily nice, nor particularly palatable. They are answers. They are meant to drive people into life with all they've got, squeezing purpose out of every moment and facing every challenge. They are the spirit of the Rebbe in a small book.

They are answers because they are for someone who has questions. Someone who experiences life and comes up against brick walls, frustrations that seem futile and pointless. This book is meant to open windows, to shine light on each of those things and reveal their meaning.

Answers are never easy; they come to those who make room for them.

People want to know if this is the way the Rebbe spoke. I've said over and over that it (generally) is not. It is my presentation of the Rebbe's world of thought—as I said above, droplets condensed from the mist. As in *Bringing Heaven Down To Earth*, I've included introductions to chapters where in some cases my own voice is more pronounced—but again, only in the presentation. If you want a book with my own ideas, you'll have to get your hands on one of the other ones. And even then, you'll likely find it's all in the presentation.

This book follows Bringing Heaven Down To Earth in that it delivers the Rebbe's thoughts in tight little packages and it presents both the pragmatic and the profound. It goes a step further in some ways. Although it is still a very practical book, you may find it has somewhat more cerebral flavor. I believe in my readers. I also believe we need that depth to tackle the world we live in today. Look, you can always choose to skip a meditation. But if you struggle with it a little, I promise it will be worth the effort.

There's another reason for including these meditations: The Rebbe's teachings are a taste of a time yet to come, of the era of light and wisdom promised in the Prophets. Sometimes those thoughts may seem very distant from our world. But by struggling to absorb them now, we are bringing ourselves that much closer to the era to which they belong.

May we be there sooner than we can imagine.

—Tzvi Freeman, Thornhill, 5766

Table of Chapters

Acknowledgements

Most of the thoughts in this book were originally written for the subscribers of *The Daily Dose of Wisdom* at Chabad.org. With their feedback and questions, I was able to polish and refine further and deeper.

Yanki Tauber, master editor of chabad.org, provided valuable edits to many of the longer essays.

Izzy Greenberg designed the amazing cover, using art from the master of virtual world landscapes, *Chuck Carter*.

Eliezer Danzinger provided many editorial comments.

Alan and Trudie Wolfish provided copious scrutiny of every detail of the text.

My dear wife, Nomi, provided inspiration, motivation and insight. Especially by saying, "Good, but you can do better."

Entrance

My mother, G–d bless her, told me there are men and women that come to this world but stay above it. My mother's mother told stories of the tzadikim of Baghdad, where she was born. If your mother never told you these things, let me tell it to you now: A world without holy men or women is a house without windows, a plastered cistern, a shrink-wrapped universe that offers no escape.

Of course, you could always paint pictures on the walls and pretend they are windows. People do it all the time. They stare at their own renditions of what is within and imagine they are seeing beyond. And so we need our precious mothers and other pure souls of simple faith to tell us, "Don't be a fool. There are windows. You can tell them easily from paintings on the wall."

How can you tell? How can you distinguish the teacher who is a window to a higher reality from the teacher who is no more than another artifact of this same old world?

The most important quality of a window is that there is nothing there. It shelters you, but it provides of itself only that which you need. If it screams out, "Here I am! I am a window! I am teaching you about the great outside!"—then it is a painting on the wall. A painting is a statement that someone felt a need to make. A window is no more than a passage of light.

There are many sorts of windows. A window could be a lens to magnify the details before you. Another could draw your vision to the details of the distant hills. There are windows to the future, windows to the past. One window shelters you from the rain that dances over its surface while another softens the rays of the sun. One looks out over a magnificent precipice, while another looks toward the truth of your own backyard. But together, it is all one view. Because all the windows share a single truth. The truth of what is.

So too, all the holy men and women, they are all one. Over the chain of generations they receive from one another, passing down a holy fire that has never been extinguished; a fire they received from Abraham and Sarah and they, from Noah and Na'ama and they, from Adam and Chava. From them we know what is beyond and where we are going, where we stand and what we must do to move ahead. Without them, we might as well be those blind creatures who are born and die beneath the earth, never to breathe from the open sky, never to behold the light of the sun and the stars. With the guidance of those holy souls, we look outside and know our journey, an amazing odyssey through a vast, fantastic cosmos.

I knew there must still be windows to our universe, that not all the shutters had been sealed. I found many paintings, perhaps a few apertures through the wall, but when I found a window I sat before it and soaked in its light, its warmth, its panorama. Its stunning revelation of what is. What is beyond and what is within—for the tiny capsule that held me had transformed as well.

-Tzvi Freeman, Vancouver, 5761 (2000)

Revolution Now

There are many ways to lie. Even an innocent truth can lie.

What did they tell you about the Rebbe and Chabad? That the Rebbe practically invented Jewish outreach and was the prime force behind the miraculous resurrection of the Jewish people after the holocaust. That Chabad is a wonderful organization with an effective strategy to reach out to Jews alienated by their Judaism and return them to tradition. That it has grown phenomenally in a few decades into a ubiquitous force in the Jewish world and in many parts of the globe has become the default Jewish establishment.

All true and so nice. And a lie.

What did they tell you about Judaism? That it's a religion with ancient, beautiful traditions. That its rabbis seek to conserve the ethics of the past and the richness of a vast heritage.

Icing without the cake, gravy without potatoes. Another truth that lies.

Abraham and Moses weren't interested in ancient traditions. They were out to create a revolution. They wanted nothing less than to change the entire world—dramatically. To transform it into something impossible.

They started the job. The Rebbe came to finish it. To arrive.

How did Abraham become father of us all? As a recalcitrant teenager smashing the idols in his father's house. And Moses? He killed a taskmaster and led a slave revolt. The prophets preached world peace and social reform at the risk of their lives at a time when ruthless despotism and dictatorship were the norm. The Maccabees fought history's first struggle for religious freedom. Akiva led a revolt against Roman government and Roman aristocracy.

Every radical idea you know that has transformed human society—the doctrine of innate human dignity, of social justice, purpose, progress, world peace, a G_d that cares about His world and hears the cry of the poor and the oppressed—you won't trace these to the Greeks or the Persians or the Chinese, but to the Jews and to the Jews alone. To the vision of Abraham that the world is not the way it is supposed to be and to the voice at Sinai that told us how to set it right.

What happened? We spent two thousand years as birds nesting in the lion's mouth. Until, when the Reformation swept Europe and the lion itself began to mimic our ways, Jewish leadership saw a choice before them: Either turn outward towards anomy and extinction—or turn even more inward, as a turtle escapes into its shell. The mission of reforming humankind took a back seat to the preservation of tradition. Where once we were driven by a prophetic vision of world peace and an era of wisdom and human dignity, now we simply yearned for relief from oppression, like an afflicted man praying for his headache to go away.

So that by the time the world seemed finally ripe to take on that vision, the only Jews to grab its horns were those already removed from the power of Torah and tradition. With rare exceptions—such as the Rebbe.

Tradition is vital, but Chabad's partisan fighters didn't walk through the fire or Stalinist Russia just so the same old past should continue into the present. Neither did the thousands of *shluchim* the Rebbe sent out to every corner of the world go there just to place another band-aid on the Jewish problem. Chabad is about a mystic view of the future—and a mystic's view of how that future will be attained. It is Abraham's vision alive today and the Rebbe is Moses playing his part in a modern, global theatre.

Now you can understand why the Rebbe met with so much friction when he spoke about the messianic era arriving soon. The outraged critics were those for whom Judaism is about tradition, about conservation of our heritage, because, after all, we've been doing these things for so long. When a Jewish leader strove to reawaken the ancient yearning of the Jew for an ideal future and claimed it's just around the corner, that just didn't sound "orthodox" to them.

In that sense, the Rebbe was never orthodox. The Rebbe was a revolutionary. And an unorthodox one at that.

For the entire text of this essay and for reader comments, visit:
chabad.org/396930

1.   A World Becoming

The times in which our generation lives are not ordinary times. We dwell on the interface between two worlds: A world as it is and a world as it is meant to be.

Everything is in place, all the infrastructure to bind the world together as one, the technology by which all of humanity can share deep wisdom, to grasp the secret of oneness with the human mind.

The stage is set.

All that's left is for us to open our eyes.

2.   UnApocalypse

This world was not created for some apocalyptic finale; its magnificence was not formed to dissipate into ionized gas. Each thing was formed for the glory of its Maker who stands forever.

Only the darkness must wind itself to its end, and it must be robbed of the treasures it holds. For the most precious things of this world are held in darkness.

That is why we must struggle with the darkness now and not run from it. All the torment it gives us, all our toil to overcome it, to tame it and to dig out the diamonds it conceals, all is with meaning and purpose.

For each obstacle that meets us on our uphill battle, each was made for the glory of its Maker.

3. What Lies Inside

Within each thing, the spirit of moshiach dwells, an
embryo waiting to break out of the shell of its egg.

In the rhythm of a dandelion shivering in the breeze, in
the eyes of the children we raise, in the goals we make
in life, in the machines we use and the art we create,
in the air we breathe and the blood rushing through
our veins. In all things breathes a dream yearning to
become real.

When the world was made, the sages say, the spirit of
moshiach was the wind hovering over all that would be.

4. Good Signs

Whenever things got worse, Jews would say, "This is a sign! Moshiach is coming!"

But in those days, a messianic era would have meant a radical change in the natural order of things.

Today, though the human soul sleeps a deep slumber of materialism, the material world itself is prepared. All the technology needed to flood the world with wisdom, the ability to feed the world many times over, the acceptance of the values of universal peace and tolerance, the understanding of the oneness of all things in practical terms—all is set in place, waiting.

In fact, if our great-grandparents in the shtetl would have heard about our times, they would have no doubt they were hearing about the messianic times.

5. Plant Now

True, we have faith that Moshiach will be here tomorrow, because he will come today in the very next moment. And if so, why build a house? Why plant a tree? Why teach a child?

But this is the journey that builds the world to come. At every stop, we do all this place demands of us. At each encampment, we build our tabernacle anew—even if just for the moment.

Each moment is an entire world, with a past and a future forever.

6. At the Threshold

At the threshold of the ultimate good, where the highest sparks of G_dliness lie on the ground before us, nobody bends over to pick them up.

Where the greatest of miracles occur, nobody lifts their eyes to notice.

The table is set for a feast, but we are all asleep—and who will wake us from our dreams?

7. Unsecret Wisdom

In the holy Zohar it is written that through the study of the secret wisdom, the final liberation will come with compassion. Not with judgment alone.

Now the wisdom is no longer secret. Sages and masters have found ways to make it accessible to all. Those who learn it and spread it, they are bringing Divine compassion and redemption to the world.

8.   Anesthetized

G_d saw the fire and the ice, the storm and the narrow
straits that plague our final journey, and He knew that
no soul could bear such pain. So He anesthetized
our souls.

Our love and fear, our sensitivity to anything
G_dly—all that was put to sleep. Only the very core,
our essential connection to Above was left intact.

There is a positive side to this frozen state: The
deepest wonders are open to us. Wonders that souls
of an earlier generation would never have been able to
approach, because they would have expired from
the excitement.

At the core of the inner wisdom lies an unbearable fire.
We walk through it today without even knowing its heat.

9. A Point Within

Within each of us is a point where all of us meet. And within that point is a place where we are all one simple essence. That is the soul of the moshiach within us.

If so, the person who we will call the moshiach does not need to convince us to follow. He only needs to awaken that sleeping moshiach within each of us. And then we will look and say, "I know this tzadik. He is the spark I feel awake within me."

That is when we will all be liberated,

we and all the creation.

10.   Day Workers

We are workers of the day.

Now is not the time to rest,

We must do what is in our hands to do,

And trust with simple faith

that our work will make the dark into day.

11.   Ethic for a Small Planet

What's needed is not groveling compliance to accepted values. A planet can't survive like that. What's needed is a restraint born of a higher awareness, a sense of the Divine. A sense of awe for what lies within another human being and within the creatures we consume. An awareness of something higher than our own minds, of a transcendence within the very ground upon which we tread.

A universal ethic born of such awareness is more than just a goal for the future. It is the only way humankind can continue to survive on this planet right now.

And it is humanity's step over the threshold of a new era.

12. In Your Hands

Meditate on a single pool left by the tide and all the life it holds. On a single leaf and all the genius within it. On all the forests of the world, all its seas, and all the life of the skies.

Then meditate that all this He has entrusted in our hands. And each person must say to him or herself: "All this He has placed in my hands alone."

13. Three Stages of Enlightenment

There are three ways of life on the ladder of enlightenment:

One is life upon a wild beast. But the inner self is awake, and that innerness is joined by a great light from Above, so that eyes stay on the road; mind, words and limbs working together to reach their destination. There are many levels to this rung, but all are within the reach of every person.

Then there is a person in whom burns a holy fire of desire for the Oneness of the Infinite Light. With this fire, he overwhelms the fire of earthly passion, until it is diminished to no more than a faint flicker. This again knows many levels, but all within the realm of the tzadik—something not every person can reach in a single lifetime.

There is also an ultimate point: Where the fire of earthly passion becomes itself a G_dly force. Then there will not be any more darkness, for we will have revealed how all darkness shines. This is the stage of a time to come, but it will sprout from the seeds of our struggle with darkness in the here and now.

14. The Dark Will Shine

There will come a time when the wolf will lie with the lamb, when the night will shine, when those who have died shall live.

But the wolf will be a wolf, the night will still be night, and the experience of death shall remain the opposite of life.

For all these, G_d made for His glory.

15. Without End

Ask the wise men of many cultures, and they will tell you that all is temporal, all will pass, there is nothing in this world to cling to, only to transcend. Ask a sage of the Torah and he will tell you it is not true. The vanities of time, the failures of life, they all pass as clouds on a windy day, but truth lives forever.

This is the meaning of the thirteenth of the thirteen principles of our faith, the belief that those who lived true lives will live again, in a real and corporeal way. It is a rejection of temporalism, a confirmation that there are things in the world that really matter, that have endless meaning and absolute purpose.

Whenever a G_dly act is performed, all involved are elevated beyond time. Save a life—you are Noah saving the entire world. Feed weary travelers—they are the angels coming to visit Abraham and Sarah. And Abraham and Sarah are hosting them with you.

In fact, all those who had truth in their lives are here with us today. It is only that we are so much a part of this river of time, we cannot lift our heads to see above it.

Only when the falseness of the world will be ripped away and all is elevated to a place of truth, then we shall all see each other, together once again.

16.   Final Sight

The angels who perceive all things from their haven above, they will never know. They will never confront the ruthless and the insensible, the mountains of obstinate darkness, the futility of screaming as mortal life flogs you against its cold, deaf barriers. To them, all things have reason, nothing is impossible, every event has its cause and that cause its cause—they will never escape the prison of knowing.

Even the G_dly soul—these are things she can never comprehend until she passes through this world. Here, cast beneath the blanket of earth's atmosphere, at some point she can no longer close her eyes to the real world He has made. And find there are things she cannot face. Things that cannot be uttered. Things that cannot be, but are.

The breath of G_d descends to this world, opens her eyes and closes them. And she will open them again. And then, thanks to her journey here, she will be able to see the Essence That Has No Cause.

17.   Pity on the Cosmos

Perhaps, for you, this exile is not so bad. An[d]
you are doing whatever you can about it,

But it is not just you. Abraham, Isaac and Jacob and all
their children through all the generations, as well all the
heavenly host –in fact the entire Creation—all is
unfulfilled, in exile and imprisoned. Even the Creator,
blessed be He, locks Himself into prison along with His
Creation. Until you get us out of here.

18.   Urgent Yearning

At the base of our Torah and our Jewish psyche lies an incessant urgency. Not just a sense that things are not the way they should be, but a relentless yearning that things should heal this very moment.

Relentless, because it refuses to decay with time or to fade with disappointment. In the morning, we make our plea as though unable to tolerate another moment. And as evening comes, we demand again as though morning never passed.

We live on the verge of eternity. May we arrive now.

19. The Now

There is no moment more vital than the one right now.

There is no space more crucial than the one in which you stand.

For this is the moment and this is the place from which the moshiach may come.

Healing the Cosmos

He pondered the Creation from every side and every angle and he realized something must have gone wrong. Something at the very beginning. Something before Time had begun and there were moments to count; before the laws of nature had been established and matter had yet a chance to form. Something at the very core of reality and if he could find it, all the cosmos could be healed.

He continued his meditations on the banks of the river Nile, his fasting, his recitation of Psalms and his sleepless nights poring over and over the scrolls of the Zohar his teacher had left him. He received wisdom from ancient souls, as had Rabbi Shimon and his son when they hid in the cave. He gazed upon the river wildlife at day, the stars of the Egyptian sky at night. He pondered all that he learned. But most of all, he pondered existence.

There is wisdom here, he thought, but wisdom gone mad. There is beauty, magnificent beauty, but she is shattered. If all the world is an epic novel, the words have been tossed in the air and scrambled; if it is a grand symphony, the musicians have lost sight of their conductor, each playing his melody on his own time. As though an explosion had occurred, blowing apart the pieces that were meant to create a harmonious world, creating instead a cacophony of melodies, a chaos of fragments.

How he discovered the secret, we do not know. A human mind, writes his protégé, Rabbi Chaim Vital, could not have unlocked this knowledge. Perhaps it was Elijah that revealed it to him; for Elijah, the Zohar says, was to reveal the deepest truths in preparation for the light of the Moshiach at the end of days. Perhaps he received from beyond even there. But when he looked in Genesis and in the Holy Zohar, he saw it clearly: *Olam HaTohu*—"the World of Chaos."

Rabbi Yitzchak Luria—also known as *Ha-Ari*, "The Lion"—was a Kabbalist, and the Kabbalist seeks a deeper reality. To the Kabbalist, the mass of humanity lives in a dream. Truth lies on a higher plane, and the Kabbalist's soul yearns to soar to that place. He separates himself from the commotion of society to sit in solitude and contemplation. He meditates until he can perceive beneath the veneer of our reality to a deeper world—perhaps the World of Formation, or deeper to the World of Creation, or even to the Divine World of Emanation beyond the angels.

But the World of Tohu is entirely beyond the finite being. It is a world emanated from the Source of All Worlds before finitude existed, before bounds were set to reality. The only bounds of Tohu are the ten luminous emanations and they, too, are without bounds. Infinite light in ten discrete modalities.

That was it, he realized. That's where things went wrong. For that is the first impossibility, where G_d comes face to face with His own paradox: His passion to be the Infinite within a finite world.

So it shattered. And that became the very core of reality: G_d's shattered dream, waiting for us to pick up the pieces.

The fire of the sun, the air we breathe, the roaring waves of the oceans and all that lives in them; the earth and the plants and animals that live upon it; even the human flesh, its vital soul and the angels above—everything we find in our world and in the worlds deeper within—all are no more than arti-facts of the sparks that fell in the explosion of that primordial world. But the essence of the human being, the breath of G_d within us, that is G_d Himself, gathering, refashioning and piecing back together an impossible dream.

He is like the father who fashions a castle from his child's wooden blocks, to say, "See? Like this!" and then to knock it all down—so that the child can build it on his own. Be-cause that is the purpose: That we should build it on our own. That we should redeem that boundless light of Tohu and fit it into the boundaries of human everyday life. For that is the only way His paradoxical dream can become real: Through those who live within it.

As for the Ari, he was like one who scales a colossal wall, convinced that a treasure lies at its summit—only to dis-cover that his prize has fallen to the mud below. Which changed everything. Because if so, the entire focus of human spirituality is misled. The greatest light, the highest beauty, is not "up there". It has fallen down here. And it is human-kind, not the angels, who can pick it up and reveal it.

Rarely does an idea so radical become so readily accepted. Yet, in a relatively short time, the teachings of the Ari became the standard reading of the Zohar. Not just because they made sense of many otherwise recondite passages, but because they made so much sense of reality and the place of Torah in that reality.

To the Jews of the East and to the Sephardic communities, the Ari has the stature of a prophet. The Chassidic movement of Rabbi Israel Baal Shem Tov that revitalized Jewry of Europe would have been impossible without the teachings of the Ari. The most common Jewish liturgy today follows the form of the Ari's custom. Even the voluminous discussions of the nitty-gritty Halacha—Jewish law and practice—are speckled with the authoritative clause, "the custom of the Ari was..."—and if that is what the Ari did, then most often that's the end of the discussion.

Not just Jews, but also philosophers among the gentiles studied his ideas and were profoundly affected by them. The profound rationalist of the 17ᵗʰ century, Gottfried Leibniz, whose ideas are only today becoming fully appreciated with advance of science, was heavily influenced by the Ari's writings—which he learned from his close friend, Count van Helmont and from von Rosenroth's *Kabala Denudata*, as did Henry More, John Locke and Anne Conway. There is even evidence to suggest that the modern idea of social activism to better our world was much due to the impact of the Ari's teaching. After all, until the Ari, G_d was the Redeemer and Man little more than a trapped fly. The Ari grabbed center stage from G_d and handed it to Man, who proactively redeems himself by redeeming his world. In a way, the Ari can be called the first modern revolutionary—for he stood the entire focus of the enlightened individual on its head.

The idea that the Infinite Light is everywhere and in everything is an axiom of the Kabbalah. What the Ari did was to make that light immanent, almost tangible, by declaring it to be held captive within every object, every event, even within evil itself.

Think again of the analogy of a jumbled text. If the Ari lived today, he would have a more ready metaphor: The email that occasionally slips through without decoding, turning up in your inbox as a jumble of nonsensical letters. You see that there are patterns, that this was meant to say something—but that meaning has been lost in the encoding.

In technical jargon, data without meaning is called "noise". When it happens in our own reality, we call it "evil". Confusion unarrested and running wild. The Ari concluded that within this evil must be the relics of that primal explosion, fragments that fell below, yet still glow from the infinite light they once contained. The sparks are G_dliness, but like we Jews, they are exiled in a world where they are out of context, held captive within their own confusion.

Evil is then an artifact, essentially fictitious, arising from the temporary state of disorder. Reorder the world and evil disappears as though it never was.

And this is where the Ari and his students after him glued together the revealed and the hidden faces of Torah, where they made the Kabbalah into an effective theology of the Halacha—and at the same time a theology of human endeavor. They asked: just how are these sparks of infinite light to be redeemed from their captivity? Where is the decoder that will return each spark back to its context, so that the artifact of evil will vanish? It is in the Torah.

Simply to find infinity within each event of our world takes no more than an objective human mind. When we perceive beauty, it is because we have found that window to the infinite. When we investigate any detail of our world as a scientist, we discover infinite information—we can continue for a lifetime and never fully understand a single organism or cell or molecule or atomic structure.

But to piece together all that infinity and reconnect it to its source—for that we must have access to the encryption code of the manufacturer. Which is exactly what we were provided when we received the Torah at Mount Sinai.

The Torah, then, is not just "G_d's vast masterplan." It is much deeper than that. It is Plan B—the plan that is only initiated once that masterplan has gone wrong. It is the plan for something greater than success, for healing, for repair.

All that the Rebbe spoke and taught was a commentary on the teachings of the first rebbe of Chabad, Rabbi Schneur Zalman of Liadi. And all that Rabbi Schneur Zalman taught was a commentary on the Ari. That is the source for this revolutionary idea you find throughout the Rebbe's teachings: the plight to find the highest sparks in the most broken, darkest corners. The idea that we are empowered to heal the world.

Whereas, the messianic idea was once all about being saved from the darkness, now it became about saving the darkness itself. It became a proactive ideal, a call to do something, something that could be found in every activity of daily life. After the Ari, the moshiach could be found anywhere.

chabad.org/296601

20. Creating a Need for Wisdom

If G_d had made a perfect world, what need would there be for wisdom?

So He left shattered vessels for us to repair. And in doing so, we engage a wisdom deeper than that which fashioned the earth, the sun and the stars.

21. Wisdom of Repair

To create is to reveal the parts from the whole.

To repair takes a greater wisdom. It is to discover the whole from the shattered parts.

He creates a world, knowing it will be broken,

so He may empower us with the wisdom to repair it.

22. Getting Ahead With Failure

There is only one thing that can put you further ahead than success, and that is failure.

When you are successful, you are whole and complete. That is wonderful, but with wholeness you cannot break out beyond your own universe.

When you fail, you are broken. You look at the pieces of yourself lying on the ground and say, "This is worthless. I must go beyond this."

Now you can escape. Now you can grow to join the Infinite. The shell is broken, the shell of a created being.

23. Breaking Limits

Everything Man is given comes in a finite package. Even the tablets Moses carried down from Mount Sinai were defined and bounded.

And so, when G_d saw Moses mourning over the broken tablets, He said, "Your powers were focussed when you smashed the tablets. For now you will receive a Torah you may extend wider than the sea."

When Man fails, he shatters the treasures G_d has put in his trust. But then he cries and picks up the shards to restore what he has ruined. That is when he discovers that G_d Himself was hidden inside. He discovers the Infinite.

24. Broken & Whole

When you find the Infinite, where will you put it? In your broken vessel? It will not stay. In a new whole one? It will not fit.

Let the heart be broken in bitterness for its confines. Let it be whole in the joy of a boundless soul.

This is the secret that Man holds over the angels: Only the human heart can be broken and whole at once.

25. Impossible Fusion

Why not remain broken? When broken, you can achieve the highest heights. When you are nothing, you can receive everything.

Because you are not made only to receive. You must also face the real world and challenge its chutzpah over and over. To do that, you need supreme wholeness, as though you were Adam in the Garden before his fall.

And if you should say, "But it is impossible! It is beyond the capacity of a created being to be both something and nothing at once."

You are right. It is impossible. That is precisely the advantage of the human being. That is why G_d created you. To join heaven and earth. Nothingness and Being. To make the impossible real.

26. Good Citizens

"Destroy Man's desire to sin," our sages tell us, "and you would destroy the world."

Not that anyone needs to sin. But one who lacks the desire to sin is not a citizen of this world. And without citizens, who will effect lasting change?

27. Gifted & Challenged

Gifted souls enter this world and shine. All that surround them bathe in their light and their beauty. And when they are gone, their light is missed.

Challenged souls enter, stumble and fall. They pick themselves up and fall again. Eventually, they climb to a higher tier, where more stumbling blocks await them. Their accomplishments often go unnoticed—although their stumbling is obvious to all.

But by the time they leave, new paths have been forged, obstacles leveled, and life itself has gained a new clarity for all those yet to enter.

Both are pure souls, G_dly in essence. But while the gifted shine their light from Above, the challenged meet the enemy on its own ground. Any real change in this world is only on their account.

28. Demands

Do you think He created us because He wanted pristine, perfect beings?

He desired that a glimmer of Himself should descend into a creature who cries and laughs and dances and bleeds; who fails as much as he succeeds; who chases after fleeting moments and is torn by figments of his own mind. He wanted to live in the petty world of such a being, and from within that place He will come to know Himself.

29.   Exploiting a Setback

Failure is wasted if you return only to the place from where you fell. If your plans fail, think bigger, aim higher.

30. Aftermath

The Baal Shem Tov taught that a sin in itself is only the bite of the snake. The real damage comes from the poison that spreads afterwards, saying, "What a worthless thing you are. Look what you've done!"

With those few words, all the gates of hell open wide.

31.   Inner Anxiety

Often, anxiety takes root because a person's external character is incompatible with his or her inner self. The anxiety may dwell upon other issues and obsessions— but none of these are the true underlying cause.

Most souls can tolerate a few inconsistencies. Others are sensitive to every nuance. As soon as some aspect of their lifestyle is not attuned to the purity of the essential self, the entire person is thrown off balance.

32. Out From Under the Blanket

Anxieties, worries, feelings of inadequacy and failure —all these smother and cripple the soul from doing its job. You need to find the appropriate time to deal with them. But don't carry them around the whole day.

During the day, you are Adam or Eve before they tasted the fruit of good and evil.

33. The Personality Thing

You need to be honest with yourself: Are these feelings of guilt and inadequacy based in reality, or just a personality issue? Does G_d really have it in for you, or is this just the pessimism of an anxious beast inside?

If it is the latter, take a break from your self-derision and nurture confidence in the Director of this universe. He carries you through every moment, but only as close as your trust in Him will allow.

As for the personality issue, channel that in positive ways. People of such nature are generally apt to serious study, deep and creative thought and dogged persistence.

34.   Hot and Cold

Fire can be dangerous

—but not near as dangerous as ice.

If a fire burns inside you, keep burning, but turn the
fire towards G_d. But if your path is of cold, lifeless
intellect, you must stop, turn around and allow yourself
to be singed by the fiery coals of the sages.

35. Redefining the Past

Nothing can hold you back— not your childhood, not the history of a lifetime, not even the very last moment before now. In a moment you can abandon your past. And once abandoned, you can redefine it.

If the past was a ring of futility, let it become a wheel of yearning that drives you forward. If the past was a brick wall, let it become a dam to unleash your power.

The very first step of change is so powerful, the boundaries of time fall aside. In one bittersweet moment, the sting of the past is dissolved and its honey salvaged.

36.   Discarding the Void

Life is true; every step of it is G_dly. Only the
emptiness is false.

There are things we regret. Things we want to tear out
of our memory, rip out of our hearts with remorse
and agony.

But in the end, the thing we reject never was. From its
birth it was not a thing, but an absence—that G_d was
not there. Once that void is washed away with tears,
there remains only a crystal jewel rescued from the
deep earth.

37. Bitter-Sweet

There are two types of events in life:

Good and very good. Sweet and bitter-sweet.

Why bitter-sweet?

Sweet, because from each event in life we grow.

Bitter, because it is so painful to tear ourselves away

from who we once were.

38. Loss

We don't like it when we lose something. We think, "What gain could there be in loss?"

But loss, too, is a way of growth.

Much of growth is simply learning to let go, to loosen the cord that ties you to your 'stuff'. Such as this thing you are missing.

Only once that is achieved can you emerge onto a higher plane, a plane open wide enough to contain more light and life than before. The divine energy that before brought a loss, can now bring—openly and clearly—a blessing and much gain.

39. Perpetual Struggle

Some think life is all about doing good and keeping away from evil. To them, struggle has no purpose of its own— to have struggled is to have failed. Success, they imagine, is a sweet candy with no trace of bitterness.

They are wrong, very wrong. Struggle is an opportunity to reach the ultimate, when darkness itself becomes light. In the midst of struggle, an inner light is awakened. Light profound enough to overwhelm the darkness, encasing it and winning it over.

But if darkness never fights back, how will it ever be conquered?

40. Vacation

When people want to free themselves from their humdrum workaday life, they go on vacation. They rent a cabin with half the rooms they have at home and sacrifice many of the conveniences they generally rely upon. They rough it. And then they feel free.

As it turns out, everybody agrees: When you let go of those material things you have become attached to, then you can start to be free.

41. Sneaky Blessings

Due to the limitations of your reality, some of your best friends can only enter incognito. In fact, the really big ones sometimes sneak through, disguised as ugly monsters and vicious enemies. Otherwise, the guards at the gate would never let them in.

These are the events optimists call "blessings in disguise."

Expand your mind, expand your world. Fire the guards, and perhaps these blessings won't need such a bizarre entry anymore.

42. Liberate Your Blessings

How to unmask a blessing in disguise:

Stare it in the face and say, "I know you are not just a lousy day or bad luck. I know you are a good friend—even if for the life of me, I cannot determine how. I know there is only one Source of All Things, and nothing can convince me that evil descends from Above. Evil descends from the constraints of my perception. You are no more than a blessing in disguise."

This blessing, if truly a great one, will not surrender its cover easily. You will need to hold your ground like a mountain against the sea. You will need a composure that demonstrates you meant every word you said. You need to surprise yourself with your own resolve.

And then you can turn over a world. A world that once distorted every blessing that squeezed through its gates will open wide. And the blessings that have already entered will sigh a breath of relief as one by one they discard their scary costumes.

43. Constructive Worrying

There are only two things to worry about: "What am I thinking?" and "What am I doing about it?"

The world around you may be in shambles—including, perhaps, yourself. Your knowledge of how things should be and what you are actually doing are so far apart, you cannot see yourself changing anything.

That's His job. He will make a bridge from your thoughts to your deeds and together they will become the most powerful instrument in the world.

You take care of your job and He will take care of His.

"What am I thinking about?"

"What am I trying to do about it?"

44. Peripheral Faults

We need a perpetual reminder that whatever faults we have, they lie only at the periphery, in the very outer garments of the soul that are touched by the ego, the persona and the world in which they are enclosed. The core, however, remains always pure and whole.

Our job then is not so much to repair and renovate as it is to unleash that inner essence. To allow it free passage to the outside, so it may take charge of our thoughts, our words and all that we do.

Even when, only a moment ago, an animal raging within tore us from our true selves—yet, in an instant, we can return with all our heart.

We are like the prince dressed in rags—at any moment able to shed them and adorn the royal garb that brings out his true being. At any point in time we can return to the essential soul that remains untouched, unblemished, unshaken from its intimate bond with the Essence of All Things.

In fact, that is truly the entire purpose of the outer mask and crust that handicap the soul: They are only there as a sort of dam, holding back the mighty waters so as to harness them, to release their power with intensity a thousand-fold.

45. Wisdom Below

People think that the truest wisdom lies closest to pure souls who stand high above the clouds of everyday life.

True wisdom is like the sun—its light must reach deep into our atmosphere before kissing the earth with its life-giving warmth. It descends like a waterfall—its most awesome power released at its base.

The deepest power of wisdom is its capacity to heal and to repair. It seeks out the darkest caverns, for there it can show off its innermost strength.

46. Stake Your Claim

Often, the person who desires good is met by its opposite at every turn.

Is it fair? It is more than fair: You cannot lay rightful claim to anything good unless you have discovered it on your own.

47. Force and Counter-Force

For every power for good in your soul, a counter-force crouches within to oppose it. There is only one place that stands beyond assault, as it also stands beyond reason or need. It is the simple power to choose good and not bad, and it is the place where the soul meets G_d and there they are one.

In that place, where that decision is made, the enemy is powerless to oppose, for it was created from that place, only to return you to there.

And you have returned.

48. Arrogance

Anger at your faults is arrogance—and of a very self-destructive form. Every failure becomes pain, every pain becomes a gruesome punishment.

Punishment for what? For having been born imperfect. As though you made yourself, as though you are your own god.

A humble person is an objective person, capable of looking at his faults, seeing what needs to change, and saying, "This is what G_d gave me to work with."

49. True Ideas

A good idea that helps no one is a lie. In the final result, it never was.

For all that is, whether earthly or divine, was only created to be part of the healing of our world, the world of action. And once that healing is done and complete, Time will look back upon itself and all it will see will be those things that made that healing happen.

In every thought, look for the power to change the world.

50. Bodily Assumptions

Why do we assume that the body is any further from G_d than the soul?

Does G_d then lie in some spiritual space outside the corporeal world?

G_d is everywhere.

51. Healing and the Mind

The worst thing you can do to recover from illness is to dwell upon it. To ponder, "Perhaps I would be better off with this remedy or with that; perhaps I should read up on what happens to people with this sort of thing; perhaps my doctor doesn't know what he's talking about and I'm going to get worse instead of better; perhaps…"

Find a good, caring doctor and follow his advice. Remove your mind from the illness and trust in the One Healer of all creatures, that He will send His healing energy through this doctor. Be confident that you will be healed.

And then let your mind rest on good and healthy thoughts that have direction and purpose to them.

52.   The Doctor

Why do we go to a doctor? Does a doctor give life?

We go to the doctor because we need to repair not just our souls, not just our bodies, but our world as well. We have made a world that brings sickness. That same world must now bring life.

53. Dual Repairs

When Queen Esther needed to save her people, first she fasted, then she went to see the king.

When something is broken below, repair it above. And know that it is never truly repaired above until it is in order below as well.

54. Healing the Other Way

There are two approaches to healing:

One is to find whatever has been weakened and damaged by illness, then repair and strengthen it.

Another is to find whatever remains viable and healthy, and support and strengthen it. Since it is one body, fortifying one aspect brings healing to all the rest.

So too, the healing of the spirit: One path is to grab the weakness by its horns and fix up your act. Another is to focus your energies on the spiritual resources that are working well. Since it is one soul, when one area is enriched the rest is elevated with it.

So too, in repairing whatever is amiss in your world:

When you see others are not doing their job, important

work is being mishandled and valuable opportunities

passed up, it is not a time for anger or despair. It is a

time for you to strengthen many times over the good

work you are doing in your own sphere.

And since we are all one, the energy you invest in your

little corner of the world pays off in every other portion

as well.

55. Love Sickness

The source of all illness is the love sickness of the soul.

She yearns to return to her Beloved Above and is repulsed by the body, her prison of pain.

Two things must be healed:

The body must be made a holy temple, for it is the place where the One Above most desires to dwell.

The soul must discover the delight of meeting her Beloved in a body active in this world.

56. Doctors

When your doctor gives you instructions for your health, listen up. If he starts predicting your fate, tell him that's none of his business.

Just as the doctor is not capable of affecting your past, so he is not licensed to deal with your future. His domain is only the present. Not *whether* you will be healed, but only *how*.

Whether you will be healed is decided in a heavenly court by your Maker. The limitations of medical science haven't the slightest influence. Your job and your doctor's job is only to allow that blessing of life to enter into the everyday world in an everyday way.

57. Doors for Healing

Let's say you ignore the need for this blessing to come into our world by natural means and just await a miracle. After all, if G_d wants you healed, what difference does a few pills make to Him?

G_d wants you healed and He wants you healed by natural means. Because if the only way to heal one of His creatures would be by miracle, then that would be an admittance of weakness. It would be a statement that G_d lives in the world of miracles but not in the world of human physiology.

When your blessings arrive, make sure there's a door for them to enter. You do whatever you can to prepare your world to receive this blessing—and the Healer of All Flesh will choose His way to send His healing.

58. Healing and Miracles

There is no such thing as healing without miracles. G_d cloaks His wonders in a series of events we imagine we can explain. But without a miracle, the best of doctors and the most proven of medicines are worthless.

When we say that a patient has miraculously recovered, we simply mean that, in this case, the miracle is less concealed.

59. Contagious Doctors

A good doctor knows that the physical health of his

patients depends on their state of mind. Therefore, he

does all he can to infect them with his own good mood.

to a doctor
who was
prone to
depression.

60. The Power of Not Thinking

Thinking has a profound effect. So does not thinking.

A mind obsessed with yesterday's travesties, today's aches and pains, and tomorrow's dark clouds, creates problems where none exist. It transforms daydreams into realities, molehills into monstrosities, innocent creatures into venomous snakes. All the more so when such words pass the lips into the tangible world we all share.

That is why simply turning your back to those thoughts is such a powerful form of healing—for every sort of illness. Divert your mind to good thoughts, productive thoughts, thoughts of confidence in the One who made you, and especially thoughts of inner wisdom.

some ask why I repeat this idea so many times.
It is because the Rebbe himself did so, and said
that healing is something of which this
generation is in great need.

61.   Advice on Thoughts

If a negative thought should arise in your mind, be still until you have chased it away. Do not allow it to pass your lips.

If that thought should continue pestering you, speak about it in confidence with someone who can empathize and provide encouragement and strength.

62. Staying Above

Your true place is a place of light. Even if you find yourself in the midst of darkness and sorrow, you must remember this is not your home. Your essential self lives in an inseverable bond with the Source of Light. From there it extends a glimmer of itself below to transform the darkness.

63. Revolution

If you were there and the Romans or the Babylonians were about to destroy Jerusalem and you had the power to do something about it, would you sit and mourn and cry? Or would you turn the world upside down?

So what is stopping you? Overturn the world today!

Where the
Essence Dwells

Every dimension of heaven was folded upon the Earth as fine linen upon a mattress. G_d was the groom, the human spirit was the bride and here they were to be wed in eternal mystic union. That was the mystery of Mount Sinai and it was then that the One Above said, "I have come to my garden, to the place I most desired from the beginning."

The angels were stunned. They had praised their Creator in sublime harmony since the outset of existence. There is no jealousy or unpleasantness amongst them, only love and brotherhood. No ignorance, no confusion, only revelation and clear vision.

They looked upon our world, a strictly bound domain where each thing grabs its place and refuses to yield to another, a place of blindness to the most obvious of truths, of savage atrocities and perverse self-destruction, and they said, "This He desires?! This He calls a garden of pleasure?! This lowest of all possible worlds, the ultimate descent of His Holy Light! This He chooses for His holy dwelling?!"

The angels are spiritual creatures, so they can never truly understand. But G_d is neither material nor spiritual—He is the creator of both heaven and earth and both are equal before him. From His vantage point, even the most elevated of spiritual worlds is a descent.

Does He then have a need for descent, for darkness? For dim shadows of beings? Is there anything the beauty of the angelic worlds can provide Him?

Rather, He created heaven and earth not out of need, not from any cause, not for any reason, but rather with a raw, primal desire: That infinite light should meet with absolute darkness and in their marriage His essence will be found.

Where is that Essence, that marriage? Here, in our everyday reality, here the Essence dwells.

64.   In the Work of Our Hands

People imagine that since G_d is not physical,
therefore He must be in heaven. But the heavens—and
all things spiritual—are just as much creations as the
earth. Less dissonant, more harmonious, more
lucid—but finite realms nonetheless.

G_d is not found in a place because it is big enough to
contain Him or so magnificent that He belongs there.
G_d is found in whatever place He desires. And where
does He desire most to be found? In the work of our
hands, repairing His world.

The heavens are filled with spiritual light. In the work of
our hands dwells G_d Himself, the Source of All Light.

65. Make Your Own Sanctuary

Ultimately, the purpose of all things is not a rational one, but simply G_d's desire to dwell in an ordinary world, the one in which you and I live. Out of His desire comes not only this world, but all worlds and all things within them.

Why does He so desire? The question is meaningless. Reason is a mere creation. G_d just is. There is nothing for Him to gain or risk losing, for G_d lacks nothing. He desires without cause, just to desire.

And what does He desire? He desires that a glimmer of His consciousness will step down into a physical body, dressing itself first within another soul, an earthly one, one very much a part of this ordinary world.

And He desires that this body and its earthly impulses will obscure and negate the G_dly light breathed into it. And that nevertheless, somehow, in the midst of all this struggle, that spark of G_d will manage to make its

mark, filtering away some of the ugliness and refining

some of the preciousness of the body, of the animal

driving it, and even of its share of this world.

This is the sanctuary that each person makes in his life,

a place where an animal is raised up in a G_dly fire upon

an altar that joins heaven and earth. It is here that you

will find G_d in His most Primal Essence, dwelling in an

ordinary world.

66. How to Be Spiritual

Let's imagine two people: Yula and Harrriet Goldberg.

Yula is an enlightened being. He spends his life in the wilderness far from humanity, focusing his mind on the higher realms.

Harriet Goldberg is a schoolteacher. She spends her life cultivating small minds, hoping to give them a sense of wonder for the world they live in.

Who is closer to G_d?

If the world came from G_d as light comes from the sun, spontaneously, but with no real interest, then Yula is closer.

If G_d created a world deliberately, because that is what He desires and cares for, then Harriet is closer.

You choose.

67.   Made On Earth

Why can't He provide simple, clear directions and let us just follow His Divine plan? Why does He place these challenges before us, forcing us to make our own decisions, to chisel out our own paths?

Because He wants a home in our world, made in our world, out of worldly materials chosen and built by citizens of this world.

But not a prefab manufactured in heaven and transported downward to earth.

68. Heaven Above, Man Below

Heaven above and the soul of Man below are two halves of a single form, two converse hemispheres that fit together to make a perfect whole.

Attuned in perfect consonance, they dance a pas de deux of exquisite form, each responding to every subtle nuance of the other, mirroring and magnifying the most subliminal inner thought, until it is impossible to distinguish them as two.

Within the human being is the consciousness of G_d looking back upon Himself from within the world He has made.

We sit upon the vortex of Creation.

69. At the Essence

Do not be misled by those who claim there is no purpose.

They may know life, but not the bowels of its fountain.

They may know darkness, but not its meaning.

They may have wisdom, but they cannot reach higher, to a place beyond wisdom from which all wisdom began.

They may reach so high until the very source from which all rivers flow. To the place where all known things converge, where all knowledge is one. But they have not touched the Essence.

At the Essence there is nothing—no light, no darkness, no knowledge, no convergence, no wisdom—nothing but the burning purpose of this moment now.

70. Tolerating Evil

If He loathes evil, then why does He allow it in His world? How can He breathe life into a world while all that is good and beautiful is ravaged by that which He hates?

It must be that His hatred of evil is not like the hatred of a mortal being for those who oppose him. Nothing can oppose Him, none of His creatures can cause Him harm. To Him, darkness is light and light is darkness, the wicked and the righteous are equal in their insignificance.

He rejects evil not for any reason, but only because He has chosen to reject these things, and that very rejection is what brings evil into being.

So too, He has chosen that those who vanquish evil will be called good. This, too, is a decision from His very essence, one that defines the very reality of things—yet it effects no change in Him.

And He quietly holds back, watchful of the drama that unfolds within Him.

71. Infinite Light

A strong light is hostile to the eyes. An intense light will burn and destroy. An immense body of light will vaporize anything, turning molecules to atoms, atoms to particles, particles to energy.

An infinite light, however, knows no bounds. It can go anywhere and enter any place. Nothing can say to infinity, "I cannot bear you! You are too powerful for me!"—for, if so, that would be a limitation on the infinite.

That is the name the Kabbalists call G_d—the Infinite Light. No place is too small, no moment too insignificant, for the Infinite Light to belong.

72.   Better Than the Sun

Some would like to be like the sun, aloof from this world. Whatever material matters they accomplish during their stay occur as if by chance, as if they were not even there.

Others fetter themselves in all the chains of life. They suffer its scars and bruises, delight in its offerings, thirst for its rewards and tremble at its pain.

True tzaddikim emulate their Creator. To them, every detail of life has meaning and purpose—every step is a decision, every move is deliberate. And yet, they remain above it all.

What is their secret?

They remember that they are not the body, but the soul.

Be as the Infinite Light: Be within, stay beyond.

73.   Investment Stuff

Look at each living being and you will see that it believes itself to be the center of the universe. It is because the Creator has invested His very essence into each and every item of His creation. And He has decided to hide within those bounds until His creation discovers Him there.

When anything of this world is repaired and reconnected to its Source, its Creator in all His essence is redeemed. And if any one thing would be left behind, its Creator in all His essence would remain captive within it.

Each living being holds inside itself the core of all Creation.

74. Purpose of a Leaf

As a young boy, Rabbi Yosef Yitzchak would go with his father on walks through the woods. They would talk; the son would ask, the father answer. And the father would tell stories of his father and his father's father before him and their fathers and teachers for many generations.

One time, as they talked, the boy absent-mindedly plucked a leaf off a tree and began to shred it between his fingers. His father saw what his son was doing, yet he continued speaking.

He spoke about the Baal Shem Tov, who taught how every leaf that blows in the wind—moving to the right and then to the left, how and when it falls and where it falls to—every nuance for the duration of its existence is under the detailed supervision of the Almighty.

That concern the Creator has for each thing, his father explained, is the divine spark that sustains its existence. Everything is with Divine purpose; everything is of concern to the ultimate goal of the entire cosmos.

"Now," the father gently chided, "look how you mistreated so absent-mindedly the Almighty's creation."

"He formed it with purpose and gave it a Divine spark! It has its own self and its own life! Now tell me, how is the 'I am' of the leaf any less than your own 'I am'?"

75. Ways of Peace

Our mission in life is not to shake up the world but to fasten its pegs; not to climb to the heavens and holler and roar, but to walk softly on the ground; not to create a storm but rather a dwelling, an earthly home for the essence of G_d.

If a storm is needed, so it shall be. As for us, we will continue on our path, the path of inner wisdom, solidly planted on the earth. A path of pleasantness and peace, bringing order to chaos step by step, until all the boundlessness of the Infinite Light is arranged firmly in our world.

76. Underrated Earth

For thousands of years, a soul waits in heaven above,
longing for her moment upon this earth only to do
another soul a favor.

Angels burn with jealousy, the heavens blush with
shame, each time an earthly human being turns itself
around and creates beauty in this world.

Heaven is nice, but on the best things, earth has
exclusive rights.

77. One World

People might tell you,

"When you come to work, leave your spirituality at home. Don't bother us with your peculiar lifestyle, your ethics, search for meaning.... That's all nice, but this is business. This is the *real* world."

There is only one real world,

and it belongs to one real G_d.

Deep Trust

It's easy to feel like orphans to this cold universe—to the elements, the forces and the empty space that shrug indifferently at the drama of being human; to a universe that answers our aspirations with a chilling silence, our failures with a blank stare. We steer our wild path through the stars as the planets continue in their set orbits, the laws of electromagnetism endure and the sun rises and sets at just the time printed in the newspaper —as though the things that matter to us most simply do not exist.

But could it be? Are we not a child born of this place? Could the womb from which human intelligence emerged truly be so dumb? If we have a heart, a mind and a soul, must not the reality that gave birth to us also have the capacity for such?

Or could it be that submerged beneath this awesome show of might hides an essence that resonates with the stirring of our hearts as an orchestra echoes the melody of its soloist; that if we could find the true fabric of reality we would find our own face reflected in its waters, our cries echoed in its depths, our joy dancing in its caverns? That we would find a universe made not of blind chance and physical law, but of conscious wisdom and the freedom that is beyond wisdom?

We believe in that essence. Sometimes we call it "G_d."

Which leaves us now with the opposite side of wonder: Does G_d then laugh? Is the Infinite Light so vulnerable as to cry over failure and rejoice in success? Does that which brings heaven and earth into existence truly love with the passion of a visceral human being or feel remorse just as a creature trapped within the tunnel of time?

But we are here, with all our inner turmoil and struggle, and that could only mean that this we call G_d desired us to be here. And when G_d desired this frail creature, He looked down from His lofty realm beyond love and laughter and passion and remorse, down into this thought of a human being, and He said, "Shall he then be alone in his place and I in mine? Is this oneness?"

So He arranged a meeting place, reflecting within the bowels of the Infinite Light the boundless emotions that are the fabric of the human soul. Like a father who stoops to play with his toddler, laughing with the child, excited over those silly things that excite a small child, yet always remaining an adult who is beyond all these games—so, too, He creates within Himself a place where in love and laughter, in compassion and awe and beauty, Man and G_d could find one another, and neither would be alone.

In truth, it is from that very place that human emotions emerge, as a child emerges from its mother's womb. And, too, in that same place, is woven the fabric from which our universe is formed.

This meeting place, the Kabbalah explains, is the place of the ten sefirot—ten modalities by which to run a universe: Conception, Understanding, Knowing, Giving, Withholding, Beauty, Victory, Glory, Bonding and Dominion. It is a place that is neither Creator nor creation, neither being nor not-being, neither infinite nor finite, but where heaven and earth merge as one—because within this place hides an Essence that is beyond all opposites, beyond all bounds.

chabad.org/391188

78. The Self-Knowing G-d

When He made the world, He decided He would take
the role of Kindness. That way, when we would be kind,
we could bond to Him with our kindness.

He decided to have Wisdom. That way, by being wise,
we could bond to Him and His wisdom.

He decided to know Himself, so that we could know
that which is beyond knowing.

79. Already Knowing

A creature born without parents can never know what it means to cry for his father and mother.

A being without a sense of the Divine can never know what is G–d and what is G-dly.

The words, the explanations, they are not meant for our minds alone, but for our souls.

For the soul already knows.

80. Mirror

A mirror is simple. It has no shape or image of its own. If it did, it would not be able to reflect the image of other things. Simplicity is what makes a mirror a mirror.

The Infinite Light from which our world emerges is also a mirror—because it is simple. Relative to our world it is a formless nothingness. So simple and void, it feels to us as though we have no source at all.

So simple and formless, it is able to reflect whatever form we choose to show it from below.

Try it. Look to the heavens and celebrate and they will celebrate with you. Look with a smile and they will smile back at you.

81. Open Wide

You can choose to fashion a G_d aloof from all things; a distant G_d that leaves you in the hands of so many worldly troubles.

Or you can believe in a G_d that carries you as a nursing mother carries her suckling infant by her bosom; as a father carries his child high upon his shoulders; as an eagle carries its fledgling young upon its wings.

Make room for Him and He will enter. As large as you allow your trust to be, so will be the space that He will fill.

82.   Not Faith

People ask, "How can I have confidence in G_d?
Confidence that He will take care of me, that
everything will work out for the best? Perhaps I don't
deserve the best. Perhaps I've already messed up so
bad He no longer cares about me."

These people have trust in G_d all mixed up.

Trust is not faith. Faith is something you may or may
not have. But trust is something you *do*. Hard.

Trust is when you are dragged by the currents of a
mighty river and you cling with all your might to a rock
you trust will not move. Trust is when, in times of
trouble, you cleave so unshakably to the heavens that
you pull them down to earth.

Trust is a mighty and heroic bonding of love. And as with all love, it is reflected in the heart of the beloved. You bond with the Eternal Rock above, and the Above bonds with you. Then you are a fit vessel for all kinds of good.

Trust changes who you are. It changes your whole world. And it is available to anybody, at any moment, no matter who they were the moment before.

It is so counter-intuitive: take control through surrender.

83. Love & Trust

Where love showers down, trust grows there, for Trust is the child of Love. And since it is a child, the reciprocal is also true: As the child's call penetrates to the inner chambers of her parents' being and awakens whatever lies still there, so trust awakens the love that gave birth to it.

So it is with a child and a parent: Provide love, trust will be born from it. Have trust and it will awaken love.

So it is with two good friends. So it is with any marriage. Your love may hibernate in a den not even you can find. But you have trust that the other holds love inside and in that trust, love awakens once more.

So it is with the love affair between your soul and her Beloved above. Trust that He is in love with you, and love will awaken.

84. Snuggle

Snuggled in his father's arms, he is secure, unafraid, because there is a father.

Looking into the small eyes gazing up from within his arms, feeling the tight clutching of tiny hands, the father awakens to something he may never have known before: He is a father.

As the child fosters a man, as he grants a father his fatherhood and a mother her motherhood, so our trust in the One Above makes Him into our G_d.

85. Separation Anxiety

Within every love, there is fear: The fear of separation
from that which you love.

A child fears separation from her parents, a lover from
his beloved, the body fears separation from the soul
and the soul from its Source Above.

So what do *you* love? Look at your worries and you will
know. If you seethe in worry over your debts and
financial future, then it is the material world you
love—because you believe in the material world and
you see it as the source of all good. If you sit and fret
over the comments of others and the glances they
throw at you, then it is social acceptance that you love,
that you have made into your god.

Cleave to the True Source Above and your heart will
have no room for fear of this world.

86. Edit Your World

Suppose we were handed a red pen and an eraser and told we could rewrite reality. If the storyline wouldn't look so nice, we could change that. Even if the outcome is what we deserve and what logically follows by our actions, it could still be edited out.

We were: Our confidence in G_d's kindness. Trust in Him, believe it will be good, and He will make it so.

Is it fair? Is it justified?

Yes. Because if you can trust so strongly, you have already transformed yourself.

87. Forget Punishment

Maybe you should be worried after all. Maybe G_d is out to punish you. Maybe He won't bother to save you from your trouble—after all, who says you deserve it?

That's not called trust. Trust means you have not a shade of doubt that He will deliver. No matter what.

88. Auto-therapy

You want to know why you deserve this series of
financial woes.

Why do you see each thing as a punishment? Perhaps,
on the contrary, it became time for you to receive much
more than ever before from Above. Only that, in order
to receive such good, you must first become small.

Like the olive, you need to come down from your tree
and be crushed to bring out your oil. Like the seed,
you must first sit in the ground and lose yourself
before sprouting and growing into a mighty oak. Like a
metal spring, you must first become small in order to
unleash your deepest power. And all these travails are
His way of helping you along that path.

If so, you already know the remedy: Make yourself
small on your own and relieve Him of the task.

In fact, you will find that you can do the job even
better—far less painfully and with immediate results.

89. Delusions of Anger

There are people who go about life believing G_d is angry with them. "After all," they say, "why shouldn't He be? I've abandoned Him. I've done things He doesn't like. In fact, I hardly ever think of Him any more. Why should He care about me?"

They delude themselves. At the core of their consciousness rests a spark of Him, awake and pulsating within everything they do. Indeed, that spark does not let them alone.

And from Above only love pours down, an Infinite love that does not change or interrupt.

What blocks entry of that love? What holds back the spark within?

Nothing more than those deluded dreams.

90. Just Do Something

You have to do *something*. What you choose is not the issue. Neither are all the neat little tricks and conniving. All that really matters is that you do your job honestly and as best you know how with the talents and skills you were given.

Don't limit G_d. Whatever the universe can provide, He is there.

91. Just the Two of You

Worry is degrading. Trust is dignified.

To worry is to worship the world. To fall on your knees
in dread and grovel before it.

To trust is to lift up your eyes and stand as tall as the
heavens. To live with nothing else but the bond
between G_d above and you below.

92. Trust Over Hope

Trust surpasses hope, as the space beyond transcends the atmosphere below.

When your mind clings to a thread of hope, it is anchored to earthly bounds. There is only so much it is prepared to receive. It is only once the thread snaps that your eyes look up to see nothing more than the open sky. And then, you can only trust.

That is Trust: When you stop suggesting to your Maker what He should do. When you are ready for surprise.

93.   De-Victimizing

Just who are the oppressors of which you are victim?
People? Institutions? The laws of nature? They are but
tools in the hand of their Master. Or are you the victim
of your own Creator?

The Designer of this cosmos does not contrive
schemes to undermine His own creations. He knows us
as He knows Himself, He sees His world from our eyes,
He is our life and our essence. When He makes
demands of us, He meets us on our own ground, not
according to His unlimited power, but finely measured
to the capacity He has hidden within us.

There are times when you compare the burden on your
shoulders to the strengths you know you have, and it
seems impossible. But He knows better the hidden
powers of your soul. And He has faith in them. For He
is there within them.

94. Fortitude

Maybe you feel you just can't hack it. You know there is nothing to fear, but you are afraid. You believe there are no obstacles that cannot be overcome, but you are unable to overcome even the pangs of your own heart.

It's true; there are people who do not run from anything, who know no fear of beast or man, of life or of death. Even as they enter this world, they remain above and beyond; their feet barely touch the ground. They are the tzadikim, those who never enter the monster's lair. But if they never enter that place, how could they ever slay the dragon?

You, on the other hand, you face that awesome fear inside on its own ground. With the power lent to you by those tzadikim, you will wrestle it to the dust. For yourself and for all those after you.

95. Know Your Strength

From your challenges you may know your strengths.

You did not make yourself. You did not choose your parents, nor did you design the environment that nurtured you.

The One who brought you to this world, who knew you before you were conceived and who fashioned you in the womb—He knew intimately all the challenges you would meet, your faults, your struggles. He was the one who designed they should be there.

For each brick wall, He provided you a ladder. For each chasm, a bridge. For each mountain, a deep reserve of superhuman strength to surprise even your own self.

When one of those challenges arises, you need only imagine what it must take to overcome—and you can be confident that just that strength is within you.

96. Hiding Behind His Hand

There are times we can catch Him peeking through the latticework of our world, filling the day with light. Then there are times when He hides His face behind a thick wall and we are confused.

He is not far away. Only that we must learn to look with a different perception. The latticework is His holy hand and the walls are He Himself.

97. Make it Your Business

In your worldly business, just do what needs to be done and trust in G_d to fill in the rest.

In your spiritual business, however, you'll have to take the whole thing on your own shoulders. Don't rely on G_d to heal the sick, help the poor, educate the ignorant and teach you Torah. He's relying on you.

Beyond Knowing

Most people have heard the story of Adam and Eve and their affair with a snake and a tree in the Garden of Eden. Few realize that it describes the struggle within every human being. Here is a synopsis of the deeper side of the story, as illuminated in the Zohar and explained by the Kabbalists and the Rebbes of Chabad:

Adam and Eve began as creatures of light. Light, for the mind, implies surrender to that which is higher and beyond, verging on anomy. As opposed to darkness, which says, "I am here. I exist." And ultimately, "All is me. There is no other."

The primal state of the human mind is a paradise of light; a state where all that matters is to reach to the light and to allow more light to enter.

There is a single temptation in that paradise, and that is to know the darkness as well. "What could be so terrible about knowing the darkness?" says the mind. "To know darkness is to know as G_d knows, for from Him come all things."

So Eve desired to know not just the act of eating the fruit, not just the taste of the fruit, but to know that *I am eating this fruit. I* as something separate from the Oneness. *I* as a meaning all to itself. *I* as otherness to the Infinite Light, as darkness.

The instant the human mind began to explore that realm of darkness, of "I am," of "Who am I?" of "How am I?" —immediately the entire cosmos was thrown into disorder. Why? Because, although Man contains a G_dly spark, Man is not G_d.

For G_d to know darkness is to create darkness. That is part of creating light. There must be beings with a sense of otherness for a world to exist—and then, into that world the light will shine. But for us to know darkness is to become darkness and to imprison light within it.

That is because the human mind is the lens of creation, where all things come into focus. Until passing through that lens, all is no more than a blur, a semi-morphous idea that could take many different meanings. It is our perception and consciousness that place bounds upon G_d's thoughts to solidify them as concrete things. In that process of resolution and definition, we define and bind ourselves as well.

That is how we become bound to the struggle of darkness and light. That is why, once the two coexist side by side in our minds, the world falls into chaos. Not a place remains as light without darkness or darkness without light. Where there is beauty, there is pain; where there is love there is selfishness. Kindness shares its bed with egotism and confidence with cruelty. In the most pristine palace of holiness in this world, the closets are filled with skeletons. In the deepest cavern of depravity, the most sublime souls are held captive. All this extends out of the confusion of the human psyche, out of the confusion of *me* knowing *I*.

When the world was renewed after the Great Flood, the Zohar tells us, Noah resolved to escape the prison of I. He planted a vineyard, made wine and drank until he had lost all sense of self-awareness. So, for him, for that time, the darkness was gone. But nothing had been repaired. So the darkness continued to grow.

It was Sarah who first repaired human consciousness. She descended into the lair of the snake, into Pharaoh's palace, into the ultimate Kingdom of Ego. There she was offered a partnership with the darkness, with Pharaoh who said, "The earth is mine. The river is mine. I created all of it. I created even myself."

Sarah, holding tightly the rope thrown to her by Abraham, arose from there untouched. She was the first to come face-to-face with the temptation of self-idolatry and walk away unimpressed. Where Eve entered into a dialogue with the snake, Sarah told him to get lost.

Therefore, the Zohar concludes, Sarah was buried in the cave where Adam and Eve lie. For it was she who granted them their first rest.

If darkness had never become mixed with light, it would have eventually found its place and become benign. Now that it has entered into battle, it has only one destiny remaining: To renounce its cloak altogether, and to reveal its inner essence. That darkness itself shines a truth that light on its own can never know.

For, in truth, the *I* can never be dismissed. Egotism is not just another nasty trait that we can grow out of. To feel *I* is to feel human; it is as much a parameter of our existence as time and space. The remedy for the *I* is not to wipe it out, but simply to put it into context.

"Yes," you say to yourself, "I have this bizarre sense that there is only one *I* and all the other billions are only *thems* and *yous*. It feels as though I am G_d, the only one true existence and all else is no more than an extension of me."

"But this is absurd. Clearly, I did not create this place. And I am obviously not in control of it. I, as all the others, am no more than a created being, an artifact of a Greater Mind. If so, why do I have this lonely sense of *I*? It could only be that my Creator desires I experience His world this way in order that I could know Him. So that I could have an inkling of knowing as He knows, so I could connect to Him with all my being."

This is the idea of the *mitzvah*: A deed that is done for no reason other than that this is the desire of the Higher Consciousness. Wherein lies all its beauty—for such a deed can only be done by one who possesses an ego.

In the darkness of ego lies the key to grasping the very Essence of G_d, for whom there is, in truth, nothing else but Him.

chabad.org/2874

more on this in The Book of Purpose.

98.   Nuclear Fission

Darkness was created with purpose, just as light. It is only the human mind that has confused the two and wreaked havoc in the world.

In this murky swamp of confusion, darkness becomes evil, for it entraps the light. When we tug to fissure their bond, an iron resistance opposes us.

But that is our mission; it was for this healing that we were given the inner wisdom, the Torah. So with every progress of wisdom and each act of beauty, we loosen that bond.

In the final release, a burst of energy shakes the cosmos.

99. Where the Self Lives

Over the years, you build an awareness of self: Who you are, what you like and dislike, how you feel about things. This is the mind of *Da'at*—a place of consciousness, of knowing and feeling "I exist." It is the most visceral of minds, closely linked to the emotions.

Consciousness is not evil. The problem is the way a human enters into his consciousness and identifies with it. What is really only an *awareness* of self becomes your *actual* self. This is the act of self-imprisonment, as you become trapped in a tight cell of self-definition.

The path of inner Torah leads you to reach beyond this conscious state to an essential self that is one with the Infinite. This is the act of liberation from a personal Egypt, which Torah makes possible on a daily basis.

100. Snake Poison

Without its poison, the snake is no more and no less than any other of G_d's creatures. Whether it be the snake of hatred, of greed, of indifference, of jealousy, of pride, of any foul aspect of human character—they are only evil because of their poison, the poison of "I exist".

Because when "I exist", there is no room left for any other being in the world to exist.

Without the "I", even jealousy and pride can be glorious animals, driving a person to greater good.

101. No Limits

The people never got used to Egypt. They never felt they belonged there. They never said, "They are the masters and we are the slaves and that's the way it is." So when Moses came and told them they were going to leave, they believed him.

Everyone has their Egypt. You've got to know who you are and what are your limitations. But heaven forbid to make peace with them. The soul within you knows no limits.

102. The Escape Hatch

All of us need a small hatch through which we can climb out of our little spaceship once in a while. So we can look at ourselves from the outside and see what is good and what needs repair and what could be put to better use. So we can look beyond ourselves and see how we compare to the vast universe. And then we can grow.

In fact, we all have just such a hatch. We don't use it much, however. Because we are so fearful of leaving our comfortable, well-defined selves and venturing into the vast Beyond.

103. Unexperience

If you can experience it, it could not be the most infinite. If you can feel it, it couldn't be the essence of G_d. The highest points in life are not the revelations and epiphanies. The highest points are the times when you just do.

When you just do, you may not feel a thing. You may not have a moment to *ask* yourself if you feel a thing. But you are one with His essence and being. You are a ray of His light.

104. Inner Torah

If you run your life according what makes sense to you, you will never be sure of anything. As good as the mind is at finding solutions and answers, it is even better at finding questions and doubts.

The path of Torah is to learn truth and to allow the Torah within you to resonate with those truths you learn, until your mind and heart and actions are guided by a voice that has no second thoughts.

105. Supermind

Intellect can orbit about the truth forever, but it doesn't have feet to land. There is a faculty, however, that doesn't need to travel to find Truth. For which truth was never hidden or obscured. For it is a native of Truth from birth.

It is not blind faith. It is an inner vision. It is not mind, but even more essential to our very being.

It is the foundation from which meaningful thought begins and with it all things resolve. For it knows intimately that which the mind can only peer at through the shifting clouds.

106. The Convenient Mind

The mind will always find the answer most convenient for itself. Even when searching for spirituality, for enlightenment, the mind will only rest where there is enough room to remain a mind. Therefore, on its own, it can never come to know the Infinite.

To reach the Infinite takes a sense that is beyond the need to exist, the essential knowledge of the inner soul. Only once the mind has drunken from that fountain can it be trusted to see beyond itself.

107. Memory

We grow because we remember; we grow because we forget. We forget 'I am this'. We remember a point within from which all forms may come.

It is the power to be all things, to not to be ruled by any of them, because in essence we are none of them.

We grow when we remember we are not what we appear to be.

108. Mind Over Heart

True, our hearts are not in our hands. But our minds are: We can think about whatever we decide to think about. And therein lies our power.

The mind rules over the heart—not just as a rider rules over his horse, but in a much more intimate sense. For the mind is the father and the mother, the seed and the womb from which the attitudes of a person are born and then nurtured. The heart does no more than reflect the state of the mind—its turmoil, its resolution, its shallowness or its depth, its coarseness or its maturity.

This then must be the focus of the person who wishes to leave this world with more than he arrived: To engage his mind with all its intensity in thoughts that elevate and inspire, and push away with equal force any thought that drags down and holds back.

And to allow all that labor to give birth through the channel from the mind to the heart to actual deeds.

109. Leash Your Heart

The mind and the heart slowly build a relationship, just as a pet and its master.

At first, the mind holds the heart on a leash. The heart screams, "I must have this! I must go there!"

And the mind says, "No, we talked this over already and we both agreed you don't need to."

And the heart screams, "But now I feel I need to! I can't do otherwise!"

And the mind says, "That's because you are a heart. Hearts feel that way. But I am a mind and I know we won't die if you don't."

Eventually, the heart learns the paths and becomes a mindful heart.

110. A Quiet Heart

The human heart is beautiful. The human heart can know secrets deeper than any mind could know. The mind cannot contain G_d, but deep inside the heart there is a place that can.

Yet there is nothing more dysfunctional than a brain controlled by its heart. At the heart's command, the finest mind is capable of the most horrid crimes.

Let the heart be quiet and hear out the mind. In that quiet listening, she will discover her true beauty and her deepest secrets will awaken.

111. Mind and Heart

The mind and the heart make a good pair. The heart is an extremist; untamed, a single emotion will fill its entire space. The mind finds balance and harmony, even between opposites.

The mind is cold and aloof. To the mind, reality is a curiosity. But the heart lives in a real world where things matter.

When the heart listens to the vision of the mind, it too learns to carry a counterpoint of voices, even the voices of other hearts. When the mind listens to the depths of the heart, then its vision can go out into the world.

112. Harmony

This is the advantage we human beings have over other
mammals: Their brain and heart are on a single plane,
but we stand erect, living in two planes at once.

We have a mind above, looking up to the stars, and
from there all things begin. We have a heart below,
pumping life into the mind's vision and drawing it down
into the real world.

When the mind and heart work with such harmony, they
make a wonderful pair. When their roles are lost, they
create an acrimony worse than hell.

113.　Panic

Panic, confusion and pessimism are the nightmares of a heart gone wild. As soon as the mind holds the heart's reins, they disappear into the night.

114. Mental Limits

Just as wisdom is not something you can touch with
your hands, so G_dliness is not something you can
grasp with your mind.

The mind cannot experience G_d. G_d is not an idea.
G_d is real.

G_d is better found through inspired deeds
than by inspiring thoughts.

115. Waking Up G_d

A spark of G_d slumbers within us, as a flame slumbers in the embers of coals.

Will she awaken from ideas? They are only more dreams to sleep by.

Will she awaken from deep thoughts? Their depth will not reach her.

She will awaken when she sees her Beloved, the Essence of All Things with which she is one.

And where will she see Him? Not in ideas, not in deep thoughts, but in a G_dly deed that she will do, in an act of infinite beauty. Then her flame will burn bright.

116. Be a Mentsch

There is a way to reach G_d by just being a mentsch.

A mentsch is someone who respects the needs and wishes of others—especially of those in his care.

In the care of each of us is entrusted a G_dly soul. She has a terrible allergy to all those messy deeds that darken her world and desires only those beautiful deeds that will bring in more light.

And you, being a mentsch, could you stand in her way?

I was there
when the Rebbe
said this
and I still
remember
the smile on
his face.

117.   The Promise Inside

No matter how much you distrust your own sincerity or question your motives, there is no trace of doubt that at your core lives a G_dly soul, pure and sincere.

You provide the actions and the deed. She needs no more than a pinhole through which to break out and fill those deeds with Divine power.

118. Decisions

Know that along with every blade of grass and every speeding electron, so too your own thoughts and decisions are directed with the same wondrous meaning and purpose by the One who created and directs all things. You only need to decide to do the right thing and His holy hand guides you on that path.

This is what confidence in the Director of the world is all about: A conviction that since He is the essence of good, therefore all things are for the good—the obvious good.

If so, what on earth are you worried or confused about? Even when your own mind determines what to do and how—even then He is there.

119. Wasting Life on Purpose

Once you have found the meaning of life, will there be enough life left to live meaningfully?

Better to live life as meaningfully as you know how, and find more meaning as you go along. You will gain and so will those you influence.

the Rebbe's reply to someone who had quit teaching to determine the meaning of life.

Scientist & Mystic

I magine yourself in the scientific hot spot of the twentieth century. At the vortex of a revolution in science such as never had occurred before, and more radical than anything that has occurred since. A small group of scientists, most of them under thirty, are rewriting the laws of the cosmos. Time and space have already been demoted from their absolute primacy, and now cause and effect are on the block.

The universe, once a collection of globs of matter following neat, well-defined paths has become suddenly much more mysterious. It is beginning to look more like an idea than a thing, more like a process than a collection of objects.

You're at the University of Berlin from 1919 until 1932, where Max Planck, Ernst Schrodinger, Albert Einstein and other giants of modern physics hold lecturing posts. Nihls Bohr and his flock of protégés visit regularly for heated debates. One of those visitors, a young scientist named Werner Heisenberg, has only recently extended Einstein's revolution past the point Einstein himself is willing to go. But the younger scientists are a dominant force after the attrition of the First World War, and their ideas swiftly gain the upper hand.

In the midst of this revolution, just as the storm has reached its climax, there enters a brilliant student in his mid-twenties, forced to flee Stalin's Russia for his counter-revolutionary activities. He is a gifted mathematician with an astounding memory, well versed in philosophy and science. He also is fluent in the entire gamut of classic Jewish thought and he is a mystic. He studies in the department of science until 1932, after which he and many of his teachers are forced to flee Germany.

In many years from now, he will become the Rebbe of Lubavitch.

To better understand the Rebbe's concept of science, a little history comes in useful. Basing myself on his letters on the topic, this is how I believe the Rebbe might tell it:

Beginning in the latter part of the nineteenth century, scientists began to apply more rigor to separating physics from metaphysics. Physics is a study of those phenomena that can be observed, measured and verified. Metaphysics is anything beyond that realm. George Mach, in particular, taught that nothing that cannot be verified in the laboratory should enter into scientific theory.

In the bag along with all the other unverifiable concepts went two rather central ones: Absolute time and absolute space. Later, cause and effect were challenged as well. This is how it happened:

Until Albert Einstein, scientists painted their theories upon the canvasses of time, space and causation. All activity of the cosmos was assumed to occur within their realm, and so science had to account for them, as well.

Einstein's genius was in great part this realization that absolute time and space are outside the realm of science. We measure space in terms of how far one thing is from another, We measure time in terms of the movement of objects in space. Whenever we measure, however we measure, it can only be in relative terms. But the framework of that movement, the absolute background, that, he understood, is metaphysics.

Had science done away with absolute time and space? Not really. Scientists had simply determined that such notions are out of the ballpark of science. Science is about that which we can observe and measure, not *that which is*. As Herbert Courant, a respected mathematician of that era, wrote, it was the realization "that science is not about comprehending 'the thing itself,' of knowing the 'ultimate truth,' of unraveling the innermost essence of the world that was one of the most fruitful turns in modern thinking."

Eventually, the revolution Einstein spearheaded escaped beyond borders he was willing to cross. In 1928, Werner Heisenberg, at the encouragement of his teacher, Nihls Bohr, and with the mathematical help of Max Born, published a paper describing his "Principle of Uncertainty." In it, he presented a mathematical model of the atom in which there are no determined states. An electron can be said to have either a specific velocity or a specific position, but not both at once.

Obviously, there is no point in talking about the present determining the future if the present itself is innately indeterminate. Science was now relegated to concern itself with probabilities rather than certainties. The solid chain of predictable cause and effect that ran through all scientific thought would have to be loosened to make way for mathematical matrices that allowed for almost anything to happen.

Of course, every scientist must have some frame of reference to an underlying entity, a "thing in itself" that is not an object of direct physical observation. So scientists develop cosmologies, concepts of what the universe really is, as a background to explain that which can be observed. But the old materialist cosmology, previously accepted as indisputable fact, was forever gone. The very concept of matter, of tiny petrified globs of indivisibly dense primordial stuff, just didn't seem to fit into anyone's observations. Slowly, scientists became aware that it never did. All along, it was no more than a secular catechism, an assertion of faith.

A prime scientist and philosopher of the time, James Jeans, remarked that the universe had begun to look "much more like a great thought than like a great machine." Later, physicist David Bohm settled for defining matter as, "that which unfolds, whatever the medium may be." Karl Popper summed it up saying that in the 20ᵗ century, "matter has transcended itself."

Ironically, it was that old materialist catechism that had been the principal ammunition against the teachings of the ancient sages. Now, with the myth of matter exploded, materialism itself had no scientific basis. By abandoning faith, science had opened the doors to explore faith. Nobody could say any longer that Science had relieved G_d of His duties. In fact, with a universe looking like a thought, a decent position for Him had just opened up—the Mastermind that thinks that thought.

So what really lies under the ocean of observable phenomena? What causes all this to be? What is time? What is space? While the scientist has a right to present his conceptions of that which cannot be observed or measured, he has stepped out of the bounds of science in doing so. He may as well be a plumber discussing medicine. True, the plumber may need medicine, but that doesn't make him an authority.

It turns out the only one way we can know "what is there" is if What Is There comes and tells us Itself. This is the Kabbalah, a revelation into the human mind of the inner cosmos and beyond. That's why Kabbalah means 'received'—it is a wisdom that cannot be attained through intellectual pursuit alone. It must be received from Above. It starts with the first intellectual being on earth, whose mind was tuned to the heavens. It was charged with greater depth at Sinai, and came into the realm of human comprehension through the Kabbalists and Chassidic mystics of the past five hundred years.

To whom the Rebbe was heir. And a scientist to boot.

120. Past the Cosmic Machine

If the cosmos were some giant machine running a procedural program with immaculate precision, G_d's involvement would be superfluous. But science has long abandoned a mechanical view of the universe. For most of a century, scientists have discussed the basic particles of matter and energy as ideas, without form as we know it.

True, science does not discuss G_d. But it does describe His works. In our times, science has allowed G_d back into the world He envelopes Himself within.

121. Fuzzy Notions

People are under the impression that Torah is about fuzzy notions, while science deals with hard facts. In fact, just the opposite is true.

Science is limited to that which we can measure. Therefore, it cannot know time and space, but only the relative motions of objects within them. It cannot know the true causes of events, but only predict the probabilities of their occurrence. It cannot know life or consciousness or love or purpose, but only measure in general terms the consequences of such.

Torah is the blueprint by which time and space and life were made. Not a knowledge that works its way in from the outside, but speaks from within and directs us how to approach it.

Torah is not science, but with the knowledge of inner Torah, scientists would have a much greater understanding of their observations of the outer world.

122. Greece Defeated

The philosophers of ancient Greece couldn't understand us Jews.

They asked us to describe our G_d. We said He could not be described. They told us that which could not be described could not exist.

They asked us to explain how He created a world out of nothing. We said it could not be explained. They told us that which could not be explained could not exist.

And so continued the debate between philosophy and Torah for many centuries. Along the way, step by step, philosophers and scientists described and explained everything they saw, until there was no room left for miracles, for prophecy, for divine providence, for G_d.

It was then that the fountains of wisdom opened for humankind and we gazed into the mysteries of the atom, of energy fields, of black holes in space.

Suddenly, the universe became once again a wondrous place. Suddenly, we discovered that existence itself could not truly be described or explained. In truth, the greatest mystery is that anything exists at all.

Today, it is okay to believe in the supernatural, for the "Laws of Nature" have been deposed from their throne. There is no reason to deny free choice, for the iron chain of Cause and Effect has been loosened. Today, once again, scientists talk about the oneness of the cosmos and a Consciousness that permeates all things.

Today, if anyone should tell you that Science has all the answers, respond that yes, it does. Its answer is to stand in awe at the design of this universe in which we live.

123. Beneath the Veneer

As science progresses, we prove to ourselves more and more: We know effects, but not cause. We describe our world in increasing precision, but come no closer to understanding why it is the way it is.

What is gravity? What is electricity? What are these forces that hold atoms together and why do they work the way they do? The scientist who pretends to answer such questions is more than helpless—he is outside of his field. He might as well be a doctor voicing an opinion concerning the movement of the stars or an astronomer prescribing medicine. Science does not have the tools to know these things, neither does it claim to, because there simply aren't any.

from a talk in 1986

Human consciousness is approaching a great realization: That beneath the veneer of order and finitude lies a cause beyond mind.

124. Dogma

Science has no room for dogma, for statements that
pretend to describe *that which is*. Exact science is
about measurements and behaviors, the tools that
make those measurements and behaviors, and the
human consciousness that observes all of the above.
This is all very, very useful. But it has nothing to do with
describing *that which is*.

from the same
talk in 1986.

Also, a letter
to the author
of a book on
relativity.

125. Inventions

In the six days of creation, G_d spoke and each thing came to be. But much also remained suspended in the realm of G_d's thoughts, waiting for the human mind to bring it into reality.

When Adam harnessed fire, bred animals and crops, and invented all the other advances of technology through the ages, he simply acted out a Divine Plan. Each creation makes its appearance at the appropriate time, all as choreographed from the beginning.

All that G_d made, He made only for His glory. Including these.

126. Cosmic Fractals

It is a wondrous feature of the cosmos, how ideas repeat themselves at vastly different scales: As planets and stars move in grand systems about their orbits, so the electrons move about a nucleus. So too the same pattern is found within the microcosm of the human being—and at every scale of every thing, from every frame of reference.

At each level there is a wholeness and a oneness, and yet each breaks down into yet more minute particles creating yet another realm of wholeness—and we have yet to find its end.

A perfect harmony of oneness from which comes an infinitude of beings. The artist has left His signature within His masterpiece, and His imprint within each and every detail.

127. All of Him

That force that holds electrons in their orbit and planets in theirs, explodes incessantly within the stars above and is the darkness that fills the empty space—that force is a single whole and it is G_d.

It is not all of G_d. It is an expression of G_d. All of it could disappear in a single instant, and for Him nothing would have changed.

Where is it that you can find all of G_d? Wherever He wishes to be found.

On the festival of Sukkot, for example, He hides within some scattered branches placed upon an autumn hut.

128. Utterly Simple

That which can be known extends according to the bounds of its form.

That which is simple becomes all forms without end.

129. More Simple

When the Infinite Light takes form to create a world, its simplicity allows it to become all things. But if it becomes all things, how does it remain simple?

This is the secret of the most utterly simple: Even within form, it holds memory of its simplicity.

And so the sages said, "He is the space of the world, but the world is not His space."

Meaning: Even the faint glimmer of G_dly light that sustains the space and form of this world, even that remains pure and simple, beyond form and space.

130. What You Need to Know

Nobody ever demanded you unravel every mystery of the cosmos, or make sense of all you learn. There are things we will come to understand and things we will never fathom in our lifetimes—as well as things that are just beyond the gray matter within the human skull.

As humans, we are indignant about such limitations, as though the unknown has no right to stay unknown. As though reality is defined by our ability to know it.

It may be hard to concede, but none of us is G_d. Our job description is not to know all things. Our job is only to pick up those truths we will each need for our mission while we are here.

131.   Ideas With No End

Every theory, every human idea, will have its limitations.

No intellect can explain that which is illogical. But even within the realm of logic, each idea is limited to its particular realm. And within that realm itself, there will always be false resolutions and/or some sort of incompleteness.

Every thought in Torah, on the other hand, is complete in itself and infinite in all its applications. A thought of Torah is as endless as the One who gave it.

132. this

What is a blade of grass?

A blade of grass is infinite light expressing itself as a blade of grass.

What is an atom?

An atom is infinite light expressing itself as an atom.

What is a universe?

A universe is infinite light expressing itself as a universe.

In each, the Infinite Light says, "I am here and I am not here. I am this and I am not this. Through this thing, know it's Maker, that which cannot be known."

133. Any Place

In every point of space, all of space is there.

After all, at the outset of Creation all of space lay in a single point without dimensions or parts. And before that it lay in a single glance of thought, scanning every galaxy, every planet, every crystal, every atom as a single whole. And so, even now, each point of space is no more than another facet of all that is.

In this way, He has rendered us masters of all space from wherever He may place us within it. On each of us depends the entire world.

I watch in
amazement a
carp
swimming in
its pond.
G_d does not
put a carp in
a pond.
G_d condenses
His infinite
light to be
expressed as a
carp in a
pond.

134. Any Moment

In every point of time, all of time is there.

After all, at every moment, He must regenerate the entire cosmos anew out of the void. And so He must renew along with this moment all of its past and all of time from its beginning to its end.

In this way, He has rendered us masters of all of time in a single moment, of the present, of the future, and of the past as well. Wherever we steer this moment now, there rushes all of time.

135. Any Soul

In every person, there lies all souls that ever were and ever will be.

After all, all of consciousness began in a single being, with a single breath of G_d within that being. And so, just as every cell of the human being contains the blueprint of every other cell and of the whole person from the makeup of his brain to the swirls of his fingerprints, so every single person contains the entire humankind.

In this way, He has rendered each of us the master of human destiny. In the liberation of any one of us lies the liberation of us all.

136. The Part, the Whole & the Essence

Each of these three things—space, time and
consciousness—can be grasped from its outside
or from its inside. Or at its essence.

From the outside, each place is its own place, each
moment its own moment, each person his or her
own person.

From within, each place is a facet of all of space, each
moment a snapshot of all of time, each person another
face to a singular humanity. For the whole is reflected
in each of its parts.

But there is also an essence to each thing, at which
point there is no distinction between the whole and the
part. When you touch the essence of any part, you find
there more than a reflection. You find this place *is*
space, this moment *is* time, this person *is* humankind.

With our minds we can reach inside a thing. To reach its
essence, that essence must speak to us of its
own—and we must listen.

Science is that reaching. Torah is that listening.

137. The Spiritual Undefined

What do we mean by "spiritual"?

The definition of spiritual is that which transcends definition. Not simply that which cannot be grasped with the five senses. We have no sense with which to perceive radio waves, but radio waves are not spiritual—because they can, nevertheless, be discretely measured. Rather, the spiritual is that which is essentially ungraspable.

True, each spiritual matter has its particular sphere that distinguishes it from another. Emotions and human qualities are spiritual, and they come in distinguishable shades and forms. Love is not fear, fear is not love, and neither of them is wisdom.

The same with the soul of each thing: The life-energy that drives a plant to grow is not the life-energy of an animal and neither one can be the soul of a human.

Nevertheless, in each spiritual entity is felt something of the other and of the source of all of them—something that is utterly simple and indefinable. And therefore, each of these things defies clear definition.

That is why the common-sense methods we come to rely upon for life on earth become a hindrance when applied to matters of the spirit. A spiritual entity remains elusive to the mind that wishes to resolve and define each thing. To have any grasp of the spiritual, you need to let go of the urge to resolve and define in tight, isolated packages. You must learn to see things in terms of relationships, directions of movement, dynamic flux. You need a mind where opposites can co-exist without destroying one another.

Which is, essentially, the mind of the human being.

138. Unapproved Truth

What distinguishes the game of intellect from the search for truth?

In both, the mind eventually finds a dead end, a state where there is nothing left to unfold and the mind must surrender, saying, "This is just something we are going to have to accept if we want to go any further." We call these axioms.

Both realize the importance of establishing your axioms and the futility of believing you can go beyond them.

It is what happens then that determines the difference.

The game of intellect says that it is up to you to accept those axioms or reject them in favor of others —because the results are beautiful or because they are unpleasing; because they are elegant or they are convoluted; because their corollaries fit so nicely into everything else you know or they are just too radical.

So that, in the game of intellect, your conclusions will be dependent upon what you want to do and what you don't want to do, who you are and who you want to be, how you see your world and how you want your world to be. The intellectual can be an industrialist or an environmentalist, a materialist or a spiritualist, a hippy or a Nazi. Intellect, with the right axioms, can justify anything.

Truth is just that which is. Something you accept despite what you want or don't want to do. Even if it is terribly inconvenient.

You don't accept Truth—Truth accepts you.

139. Experience First

It is liberating, this knack we have to discover what works before understanding how.

Certainly, it is nice to know the 'how'. When you know and understand, you can immerse your entire mind and heart into the matter.

But when you experience that which you do not yet understand there is surprise and there is wonder. For that moment, you are swept away and lifted out of your little world. You taste first hand that, yes, there is truly a reality that exists beyond my own mind and heart.

This is the path of wonder the Torah takes to come into our world. It is a path that takes an open mind, one ready for truths beyond itself. As the people declared at Sinai, "We will do, and then we will understand."

140. Surrender & Conquer

The mind that demands all things enter its realm will contain nothing. The mind that allows for knowledge beyond mind will contain everything.

Every theory has a premise, every explanation an assumption. Every wise person prefaces his pursuit of wisdom by acknowledging, "This I will not be able to explain. This will remain in wonder."

Tear off a piece of your bread before you eat. You cannot fit it all into your mouth.

Do the same with wisdom. For Truth does not begin with Mind.

141.   The G_d-Point

G_d is found in nature, and He is found in the miraculous—but He is neither the laws of nature, nor is He the miracle.

He is found in matter and He is found in spirit—but He is neither matter nor spirit. He is found in heaven and He is found on earth—but He is neither heaven nor earth.

He is found in the soul and in the body, in form and in matter, in the righteous and in the wicked, in light and in darkness, in existence and in the absence of existence—

He is found in all things and in all opposites, yet He is none of them. At the point where all of these opposites converge, look there for G_d.

That is why G_d's name is Peace. When each retains its own uniqueness, yet all converge in harmonious union, there dwells G_d.

142. Within and Beyond

There are two vantage points for G_d:
Within and Beyond.

'Within' is the view of the created, fixed within a defined reality, consumed with its own importance, where things matter and life is real.

'Beyond' is the view of the Creator, detached and transcendent. Where all that has begun has already ended, nothing can assert its significance, for all is nill.

There is also an Essence of both Within and Beyond, neither subject to the narrow view of a finite being, nor biased by the detachment of the Infinite. Neither created nor Creator, neither below nor Above, neither existence nor its absence.

It is the Essence, both Beyond and Within all things. Beyond, because it needs no purpose. Within, because it nevertheless chose one.

Both Within and Beyond breathe with that purpose, the purpose of their very being: That the Essence be revealed from Within.

143. Deliberate Life

At every moment the sun keeps shining—or else life on our planet could not continue. So too, at every moment the Creator renews the very existence of His creation.

There is a distinction, however: The sun supports life spontaneously. It is not concerned, nor interested —nor even aware of the blade of grass that grows from its warmth and light. It is only being itself—a giant atom crusher in the sky—and we benefit here on earth.

Creation, on the other hand, is intentional. Every step along the way is a deliberate act, every detail is with intimate concern, every event is judged, decided and accounted for. He vitalizes each thing not only with His light—but, like an artist, with His entire Being.

And yet, He remains unchanged—like the sun above, and infinitely more so. Immanent, yet transcendent. For He knows no bounds.

144. Without Cause & Effect

Each moment of the present contains a myriad possibilities for the future—that is all the so-called 'Laws of Nature' provide. There is no chain of cause and effect, no predetermined fate. It is not the present that determines the future. It is us.

If it seems otherwise to our eyes, that is only because we do not perceive the world as it is outside of us. We perceive a world that we have already touched, that our knowledge can fathom. But the true world is beyond anything we can comprehend. It's very nature is G_dliness.

And therefore, anything could happen next.

145. A Safe World

At one time we thought human ethics could care for the world. "Human intelligence," we argued, "will find truth and protect it."

We discovered we were wrong. The nation that cultivated the human mind to its highest degree committed the most horrifying crimes of our age. Human intelligence today has not saved the world, but ravaged it.

The world cannot survive without a foundation deeper than anything it contains of its own. These are the laws that Noah heard and passed on to all humanity, based on the faith that there is a Creator Who cares about His creation.

I & Other

This is the impossible position in which He has placed us: We believe that at the core of reality there lies a G_d who is essentially good and cares for each one according to his or her needs, guiding each one to the right path, punishing wickedness and rewarding goodness in fair and equal measure. And so, over and over we are outraged—because what we experience flies in the face of this entire belief.

Yet, if we abandon either pole, we might as well have never been born: If we learn to ignore the existence of the evil and the suffering, finding some justification for G_d or simply hiding our heads in the sand—then for what purpose were we placed in such a world? To leave it as we found it? And what kind of a G_d have our justifications created?

But if we should surrender our G_d, concluding that, "there is no Judge and therefore no justice"—then what value does my life have? What value does any life have? And so what is the point of all the outrage?

This is the drama created by a G_d entirely beyond any form of understanding—a drama powered by the agonizing tension of paradox.

They asked the Baal Shem Tov, "The Talmud tells us that for everything G_d forbade, He provided us something permissible of the same sort. He forbade us to eat blood and permitted the liver—which is full of blood. He forbade the mixture of milk and meat and permitted the cow's udder. If so, what did He permit that corresponds to the sin of heresy?'

The Baal Shem Tov replied, "Acts of kindness."

Because when you see a person suffering, you don't say, "G_d runs the universe. G_d will take care. G_d knows what is best." You do everything in your power to relieve that suffering *as though there is no G_d*. You become a heretic in G_d's name.

chabad.org/274117

146. The Image

How you treat others is how G_d treats you. How you forgive them is how He forgives you. How you see them is how He sees you.

When you show empathy for the plight of another human being, G_d takes empathy in your plight.

When others slight you and you ignore the call to vengeance that burns inside, G_d erases all memory of your failures toward Him.

When you see the image of G_d in another human being, G_d reveals His image within you.

147. Only You

All this universe was made only for your journey. And all this universe was made only for the other guy's journey. And for mine as well.

In our mind it is impossible. We are finite. When we put our heads to one idea, there is no room for any other. If one point stands at the center, there is no center left in which another could stand.

But G_d is infinite. He can have as many points of focus as He wishes without diminishing the centrality of any of them in the slightest.

Each one of us is absolutely the most important thing in the universe.

148. To Love

To love is to sigh at another's sorrow, to rejoice at another's good fortune.

To love is the deepest of all pleasures.

149. What is Love?

Two people live together, care for each other, weather the storms together

—and one day they discover they cannot live without each other. That is love.

You don't fall in love. You create love.

from an
exchange with
a young
woman who
was looking
for her white
knight

150. Deep Love

You cannot reach deeper within another than you reach within your own self.

If you love yourself for your achievements, your current assets, the way you do things and handle the world—and despise yourself for failure in the same—it follows that your relationship with another will also be transient and superficial.

To achieve deep and lasting love of another person, you need to first experience the depth within yourself —an inner core that doesn't change with time or events. If it is the true essence, it is an essence shared by the other person as well—and love can only follow.

151. Compassion

What is the difference between kindness and compassion?

Kindness gives to another.

Compassion knows no 'other'.

152. Getting Along

When we can't get along with someone, we like to blame it on that person's faults: Stupidity, incompetence, outrageous actions, aggression or some other evil.

The real reason is none of these. It is that the world is broken, and we are the shattered fragments.

And all that stops us from coming back together is that we each imagine ourselves to be whole.

153. Working It Out

Every idea has many applications. When you find
yourself in disagreement with a friend, look beyond
your positions to the idea within them—perhaps it is
the same one. If so, you should be able to find a third
application which satisfies both your needs.

154. Aid Your Nemesis

You may have real reason for disliking someone. He may be a bad influence. He may be corrupt and decrepit.

But if he needs a favor—as long as he is not destructive—go out of your way and do it for him.

First of all, he is still your brother. Secondly, you'll be a better person for it.

155. Love Pulls

There is only one way to bring people closer to truth, whether your friend, your spouse, your child, or a complete stranger.

It is not with rebuke, not with arguments, not with intellectual games—but by drawing them with thick cords of love, by showing your faith in who they are.

And with real deeds.

156. Unfailing Love

Love can fail, and we must know that it can fail. For if love was always reciprocated, how could there ever be sincere love?

Rather, every person retains free will. No matter how strong you pull him onto the right track with cords of love, he may always turn his back and run away.

But you have done your part, you have shown love. And what is the reward of the mitzvah of love? That your soul and his ascend to a higher plane and the Infinite Light gains a window to enter this world.

Which is really all there is.

157. Appropriate Criticizing

Criticizing another person is not out of the question. It's just that there are a few conditions to attend to before you start:

First, make sure this person is your close friend. Those are the only people worth criticizing—not just because they may actually listen, but also since you run a lower risk of making them into your sworn enemies.

If this person is not yet your close friend, you'll need to spend some time with him, finding out everything that's good about him and going out of your way to help him out until a real friendship develops.

Also, you'll need to ensure that this person has the same knowledge, understanding and perspective of right and wrong as you do before you can attack his decisions. If he doesn't, you'll need to spend some time learning and discussing together until you see each other's point of view.

Once the two of you are in the same headspace, and he's your good friend to boot, then it's okay to criticize—if necessary. And if you can remember what there was to criticize.

158. How to Criticize

If you have not yet succeeded in fulfilling the criteria mentioned above, yet still feel a necessity to provide criticism, there is an alternative:

Sit and criticize yourself, very hard, from the bottom of your heart, until the other person hears.

If it comes from your heart, it will enter his as well.

159. Rebuke

By the time Moses returned to the scene, his people had hit an all-time low. Perhaps he should have told them off, saying, "Repent, sinners, lest you perish altogether!"

But he didn't. Instead, he told them how G_d cared for them and felt their suffering, how He would bring about miracles, freedom and a wondrous future out of His love for them.

As for rebuke, Moses saved that for G_d. "Why have you mistreated your people?!" he demanded.

If you don't like the other guy's lifestyle, do him a favor, lend him a hand. Once you've brought a few miracles into his life, then you can urge him to chuck his bad habits.

160. Do-it-yourself Lawyer

As thinking human beings, we have an unlimited capacity to find excuses. To discover ingenious and innovative ways to distance the perpetrator from the act.

We can blame it on youth, on old age, on parents, on children, on financial hardships, daily environs, psychological state. We can easily discharge anybody of any responsibility for any negative deeds that stain their hands. We can all be wonderful advocates and lawyers for one another—and the Merciful One Above surely enjoys hearing such things.

But if you want to get ahead in life, don't be your own lawyer.

161. A Woman's Way

A woman's influence is very different from a man's. A
man needs to dominate, to conquer and vanquish an
opponent. His victory is all about appearances—he
may get the other guy to nod his head, but not
his heart.

A woman, however, reaches inside a man, so that he
may not even recognize her influence. He feels as
though this was his idea all along.

There is still hope for men, since they can learn this
method—to a degree— from women.

162. Man & Woman

It is a mistake to consider man and woman two separate beings. They are no more than two halves of a single form, two converse hemispheres that fit tightly together to make a perfect whole. They are a single universe, heaven and earth encapsulated in flesh and blood.

It is only that on its way to enter this world, this sphere was shattered apart. What was once the infinity of a perfect globe became two finite surfaces. What was once a duet of sublime harmony became two bizarre solos of unfinished motions, of unresolved discord.

So much so, that each one hears in itself only half a melody, and so too it hears in the other. Each sees the other and says, 'That is broken.' Feigning wholeness, the two halves wander aimlessly in space alone.

Until each fragment allows itself to surrender, to admit that it too is broken. Only then can it search for the warmth it is missing. For the depth of its own self that was ripped away. For the harmony that will make sense of its song.

And in perfect union, two finite beings find in one another infinite beauty.

163. Feminine Bread

There was a time when a woman's charity was valued more than a man's. A man gave a pauper coins, which then had to be exchanged for food. A woman would just take a loaf of bread out of her oven, warm and ready to eat upon delivery.

The distinction lives on today in other terms: A man's way is to serve your impoverished soul ideas— perhaps you will be wise enough to translate those ideas into deeds. But a woman goes straight for the heart and guts. She tells you, "This is who you are and this is what you must do to be who you are."

164. Intolerance

Intolerance lies at the core of evil. Not the intolerance that results from any threat or danger. Not the intolerance that arises from negative experience. Just intolerance of another being who dares to exist, who dares to diminish the space in the universe left for you. Intolerance without cause.

It is so deep within us, because every human being secretly desires the entire universe to himself. Our only way out is to learn compassion without cause. To care for each other simply because that 'other' exists.

165. Putting Modesty Aside

In general, modesty is a good trait. You're far better off concealing your talents and good deeds in the shadows.

But when you come to the defense of truth and justice, then is a time to stand up and make yourself heard loud and clear.

As for your modesty—you'll just have to put that aside for the moment.

166. Words of the Other

If you have spoken to another and your words did not help, it is proof you did not speak with him but with yourself. Your words may be the words you wanted to say, the words you believe, but they are not the words he needed to hear. If you would speak to him and speak his words, then certainly he would hear.

167. The Sung Unhero

Your most heroic acts are those you may not even be aware of.

Like the time you could have gotten even with the guy in the next cubicle, and nobody would have known. And you really wanted to. But you didn't, just because it's not right.

You may not have been impressed—you may even have been disappointed with yourself. But the angels burst into song, as all your world rose up a niche. It may have been the most elevating act of a lifetime.

Heroic acts are wonderful, but that could be just your nature. When you break out of your nature, you enter the realm of the G_dly.

Mastering Your World

" If life is full of meaning, why am I spending it hustling other people for their money?"

Don't think the question was invented by our bourgeois-bohemian, save-the-world-and-get-rich generation. It's been around since G_d handed Adam a hoe and kicked him out of the garden. Just that most of Adam's children worked that hoe with their hands. Today, we are all plowing the earth with our heads. And that can mean some pretty muddy heads.

Some of us like mud. Some think mud is disgusting and run away from it. A lot of us try to compromise—we'll just get a little bit dirty and try to wash up often. In which case, we end up with a bifurcated life in which our principal occupation is making money and finding meaning is a pastime.

What we really want is a way to have it all. We want to discover that selling widgets is actually a path to higher consciousness and that true enlightenment doesn't have to be accessed in serene meditation remote from humanity

—you can grab it from a corporate desk overlooking downtown Atlanta. Maybe even a law firm.

But if widget sales are all about getting hold of other people's money, then how can there be any nexus between this and your personal spirituality?

We have to re-examine what business is all about. Perhaps business, too, is about discovering meaning. About discovering jewels in that mud.

The master Kabbalist, the Ari, contemplated our question five hundred years ago—but on a more basic level: If man is a spiritual being, why must he eat? Animals, it would seem, are less spiritual than people. Vegetables seem even lower—and the earth, air and sunshine would appear to be at the rock bottom. Yet vegetation is nurtured by those elements, animals are nurtured by both those elements and the vegetation, and human beings rely on all three. Why, the Ari asked, is the pyramid turned upside down?

Or maybe it's not upside down. Maybe, in some way, those animals hold within them a divine spark that is far beyond anything a human can attain on his own. Maybe the deeper you go into the earthiness of planet earth, the brighter the sparks become, so that the greatest sparks are found in the earthiest places. Which means that the real reason we eat is not for ourselves, but for the sake of our food. To uncover those sparks and connect them back to their source—and to one another.

Which is just what the Ari and his students taught: That all of human endeavor is meant to be a way to reconnect the world and reveal its G_dly power.

There is a caveat, however, to this process: In order to rescue a spark from its captivity within your food, you need to stay one step above it. If you're "grabbing a bite," the bite is grabbing you. Meaning that if it's the food that's demanding, "You need me. You must eat me. Eat me now!" and you stoop and obey—then it's not the spark that's being lifted up, but you that's being dragged down. Eating, the Ari explained, must be treated as any other spiritual activity, with composure, with mindfulness—as a human being.

Just as Adam with that hoe uncovered the power of the earth to produce bushels of food, so the widget seller has discovered a way to enhance human life with a simple array of wires and plastic. The systems analyst, too, is constantly in the process of digging value out of the abyss into which it has fallen. The orthodontist uncovers enhancement to human life so that no young lady need go without a pretty smile.

Turns out that business really is about finding meaning—about finding and exposing the secret power of the world around us. And not only the power to enhance human life, but also the power of miracles and wonders and beautiful deeds. The infinite light hidden in finite places.

The widget guy found that infinite light hidden in an inner city school, when he realized how his widgets could be used as a tool for teaching cooperation and literacy. The Atlanta executive revealed it in his own office when he arranged for a weekly lunch 'n learn session with a local rabbi who discusses Talmudic business ethics. As for the orthodontist, she finds it every day, in the wonderful smiles she brings to young girls, especially the ones from underprivileged families, who she takes as patients without charge.

The deeper we enter the caverns of mundane life, the more brilliant are the jewels we find—as long as we stay above while we enter within. Meaning: As long as we remember that the purpose of our occupation is not the obvious one of making money, but a deeper, higher purpose. Because we are all, in truth, spiritual beings navigating a material world.

As the Psalmist writes, "Those who go down in ships to the sea, who do their craft in the mighty waters; they are the ones to see the works of G_d, catching His wonders in their net."

chabad.org/377329

168. Unslavery

It is not business, not money, nor career, nor human relationships that tears our souls from us and us from our G_d.

There is as much beauty in any of those as there is in any flower from the Garden of Eden; as much G_dliness as in any temple.

It is the way we lock ourselves inside each one, begging it to take us as its slave, refusing to watch from above, to preserve our dignity as human beings.

As you enter each thing, stay above.

169. Re-piecing

At first, all existed as a single whole in a single thought. Then it fell below, shattering into tiny fragments and fragments of fragments. Now Man picks up the pieces and says, "This seems to belong to this, and this relates to that," until he reaches back to the whole as it was in primal thought.

It is not the cause and why of things that we find. Things are the way they are because that is how their Maker decided they should be. That is beyond the domain of intelligence. The beauty of intelligence is that it finds the harmony and elegance of the whole as it was originally conceived.

170. The Puzzle

Think of your world as a massive jigsaw puzzle in time and three dimensions. All the objects and events are meant to fit together neatly, yet they seem just a heap of dysfunctional fragments.

Here is the trick to reassembling those fragments: Find your own purpose first and start moving headstrong towards it. Once in that mode, all things related to your purpose will find you. And those things already attached to you will find their place as well.

Suddenly, where once noise and chaos tore you in a thousand directions, a great symphony occurs.

171.   Investing in Earth

The soul descends to an earthly realm and a material body because she sees what can be achieved there—heights she could never attain by remaining in the realm of the spirit.

That is why we take care of ourselves, our families, our fellow human beings and our lovely planet earth. Not out of fear or dread or panic. But out of knowledge that within each of those things is a beauty the highest of angels cannot touch.

172. Two Decisions

Standing at the threshold of Creation, He determined two things:

I will be involved in every detail.

I won't be found in that place until they invite me in.

173. Chutzpah

The first thing you must know before anything else applies: Truth demands chutzpah.

If what you are doing is the right thing to do, there will be others who will ridicule, taunt and attempt in every way to intimidate you. That is the way the world works.

If you can't handle it, if you can't ignore them as you would ignore flies on a camping trip, don't imagine you can take a single step forward.

Only once you've passed the chutzpah test, only then can you begin to grow.

174. Just Go Over It

For each problem, look for the crux of the issue and find the most direct, simple and powerful solution. The solution that pulls the rug out from under the feet of the problem and leaves it no room to return.

This solution will likely also be the most outrageous. That's okay. You'll do it in a perfectly natural way, as though this is just the way things have always been done. Don't bat an eyelid and hope no one else will.

175. Naturally Outrageous

When G_d desired to create the world, He went for the most outrageous solution. With the power of His very Essence, He burst it into being out of the absolute void. And He continues doing so every moment.

He could have done things otherwise. He could have taken an orderly approach and allowed a creation to gradually evolve, while staying aloof and beyond the whole thing. Even though that doesn't make sense to us, He could have made a universe with a different set of logic so that it would have made sense.

But as it stands, the world was created with an outrageous solution. That is why such solutions tend to be the most natural ones to this day. With all your essence, go for it head-on.

176. Enter High

Never squeeze yourself into this place called world out of fear.

Enter with your head high, as a soul with a lofty mission.

177. Release

Beginnings are hard—and for good reason. If they were easy, we would prowl into each new venture like a smug, fat cat.

When you begin pent up in an iron cage, a new life emerges. A tiger that breaks through the door of its cage and pounces with a vengeance.

Bless those cages, those impossible brick walls, those rivers of fire that lie at the outset of each worthwhile journey. Without them we would be only as powerful as we appear to be.

178. Opponents

Opponents are evidence that you are moving forward.

Their power comes from your fear of them.

*from a letter to a shliach
(a representative of the
Rebbe)*

179. Adulthood

Three things you must know to be an adult:

Don't fool yourself.

Don't fool others.

Don't let others fool you.

—and do it all without trying to impress anybody.

Rabbi Sholom Ber
told this to his son
before his
bar mitzvah.

180. Flattening the Ride

When business is down, envision yourself tomorrow when all the efforts of today have succeeded and you sit before a table set with all your needs.

When business is up, pray for your livelihood at every step as a beggar prays for his daily bread.

For everything is in His hands.

181. Supply and Demand

Time, too, has its geography.

There are times when the scenery is ordered in monotonous rhythm. Times when nothing new knocks on your door for weeks on end.

And there are times when nothing will rest in its place for a moment, hostile terrain defies your every step and a torrent of demands pounds relentlessly down .

There is a mechanism behind these seasons of Life: Above, the energy of life throbs in continual metamorphosis as the portals of heaven expand and contract. At times, the energy of life is metered out in rhythmic doses, precisely according to what the world can contain. At other times, those portals open wide, so wide that the soul is overwhelmed with sudden light. In our world, life overflows.

There is only one thing to remember: Do not fear the rush of light. Just as He adjusts the flow, so He empowers His creatures to receive it.

When the rivers of life overflow, so do your powers to traverse them.

182. Seasons of Essence

There is the body, the soul, and then there is the essence. If the soul is light, then the essence is the source of light. If the soul is energy, then the essence is the generator. It is not something you have. It is who and what you are.

Whatever we do, we dance around that essence-core, like an orbiting spacecraft unable to land. We can meditate, we can be inspired -- but to touch our inner core, the place from whence all this comes, that takes a power from beyond.

That is why there are seasons in life empowered from beyond. Special days and special nights, times of crisis and times of joy that touch the core. At other times, you can step forward. At those times, you can leap into a new form of being.

183. Life in a Day

A day is more than a passage of time. A day is a passage of life.

Before you were formed in the womb, your days were numbered and set in place. They are the chapters of the lessons you came here to learn, faces of the wisdom this world imparts, gateways to the treasures that belong to this lifetime alone.

Each day enters, opens its doors, tells its story, and then returns above, never to visit again.

Never—for no two days in the history of the universe will ever be the same.

184. Dissatisfaction

Some people tell you that if you're never satisfied with your achievements, you'll drive yourself nuts.

Ignore them. Look at whatever you've done and say, "If that's good, double is better."

Don't let what you've done be the final measure of who you are.

someone wrote that the Rebbe had said we should 'never be satisfied with our past achievements.' The Rebbe crossed out the word 'past'.

185. Perpetual Freedom

No man can say he is free today because yesterday he was granted freedom.

Freedom is a source of endless energy. Freedom is the power behind this entire universe. Freedom is the force that brings existence out of the void.

You are free when you take part in that endlessness. When you never stand still. When you are forever escaping the confines of today to create a freer tomorrow.

186. The Human Untied

No one can predict the tomorrow of a human being. We move from abject poverty to opulent wealth on the spur of a moment, from hedonism to spiritual heights in a sudden flash. We are creatures who know no bounds, with limitless power to be whatever we want to be.

We get stuck—but not from a shortage of power. Rather, it is from our failure to recognize the knots with which we have tied ourselves.

187. Wake the Day

If you are awake just because it is day then you are still asleep. The sensation of wakefulness—that is just the day suspending you above your bed. But the 'you' inside still slumbers.

Wake up in the morning and tell the sun to rise. Decide what sort of a day it will be and make it happen.

188. Awake at Night

Just as we learn to walk by falling down, so we learn to
be awake by groping in the dark. When there is no
support, no brightness to keep us on our toes, when
we are all on our own, that is when we learn to be
awake. Truly awake—not because it is day, but
because we are awake.

189. The Oppressive Neighbor

No one is a greater tyrant than your friendly neighbor.
Or fellow workers at the office. Or friends at the gym.
The mere anticipation of their scrutiny arrests all
growth before it can even germinate. "Why have you
changed your way of life? Was everything you did until
now wrong? Why do you feel a need to be different?"
The most tyrannical regime could never be as
oppressive.

The secret is: they may never even make a comment.
They probably don't even care. So where do all those
intimidating questions come from?

They come from your own little tyrant inside.

190. Self-Oppression

A tyrant can steal everything from you but your knowledge of who you are. That only *you* can give away.

When someone else imprisons or enslaves you, you still know who you are—even if you are prevented from expressing it.

When you make your goal in life to become someone you are not, or to belong to that which your soul rejects, that is the ultimate surrender. There is no greater captivity, for your essence and being have been locked away in a dark cell.

It is an oppression of the worst sort, but also the easiest to escape. After all, you admitted yourself into this place. So who is preventing you from signing out?

191. From Moses to Now

Moses fought the oppressor and at the last moment taught his people to be free.

Today the oppressors are much subtler. We need to teach people to be free so that they can recognize their oppression.

192. Healthy Contributions

A team, a society, a world is healthy when each member says, "If I don't add in my two bits, the whole system will fail."

Not just any two bits, but the two bits that belong to that individual in particular.

Nothing can be allowed to just serve another. Nothing can function only according to instructions. For each thing has a spark of the Divine.

193. Natural Desire

It is natural and healthy to want material things. If nobody cared about material things, the earth would be desolate. But there's no need to burn inside over them. That is beneath the dignity of a human being. And it eats away your passion for the more important things in life.

Save your fire for those things central to your purpose of being. Boston cream pie and shiny Lambhorginis are not central to your purpose of being.

194. Unnatural Desires

The natural desires with which we were born are all meant for good and healthy purposes. But the human being has a knack for creating desires that contradict his essential nature. Desires that are destructive to himself, his society and his environment.

You can't channel such desires. You need to wipe them out and start again from what G_d gave you.

195. The Prison of Stuff

The stuff you own owns you. You put your soul and being into acquiring it. Your heart jumps at the thought of it disappearing. It is the tether that ties you to the ground.

You could give it all away and lead an ascetic life. But you will be no more than a coward. A slave who runs away is still a slave until he becomes his own master.

Here's how to become your own master: Each time money comes to you, show it who's boss. Prove you hold the power to set it free. Tear off a piece for someone in need.

Keep the rest and use it for good things. You are no longer its captive. When the piece you gave away rose to the heavens, all that you owned rose also and was transformed.

196. Standing Up

There are times an urge burns so fiercely inside, it becomes a taskmaster with a stinging whip. From where does darkness attain such awesome might to consume the power of a G_dly soul?

It is not its own power—for darkness has no power of its own. Darkness is no more than the absence of light, and your soul is pure light.

It is a power G_d has granted to the dark on a temporary understanding, so that it may challenge the human soul and awaken its innermost depths.

That is why, as soon as you will stand up and say, "My soul is not the chattel of any taskmaster! I have free will to choose as I please and I choose life!"—before that instant is over, the tyrant inside is no more, as shadows vanish before the light.

197. Normal Miracles

These things people call amazing coincidences, synchronicity, small miracles—this is the way the world is *supposed* to work. It is only that the world is in slumber, like a sleeping person who does not see, does not hear, does not speak— so that nothing distinguishes his head from his feet, his heart from his brain. So too, the world lies deep in a dream where anything is possible, but nothing seems to have a goal. Where only chaos reigns.

It takes only one person to open his eyes, his ears, his mind and his heart—and the objects of this world fall into place and work together as a single whole. Synchronized. As they were meant to be.

198. Miraculous Failure

An open miracle is somewhat of a failure for G_d. Once all is said and done, He got His way only by ignoring the norms of our lower world, by breaking His own rules. If He can perform miracles only by bullying Nature, He may as well concede that our world is a place the Infinite Light does not belong.

So He also makes another sort of miracle—the sort that blend seamlessly into the order of things below. These are impossible miracles: They break no rules, but change everything. In truth, they are the most awesome of miracles—these that reveal the Infinite unrestrained within the nature of everyday things.

199. The World At Your Feet

Why are the lives of the sages filled with miracles?

Whoever opens his mind to Truth and labors over it day and night, he is the awakened mind of the cosmos—for through him the Infinite Light enters this world. And so, nature bows to him, the angels wait upon him and everything is arranged to serve his mission.

200. Self-Made Exile

Nothing is larger than the decision to do good. Nothing is more powerful than the study of Torah. When you are occupied in these things, the whole world becomes a mere backdrop, there but to stage your actions.

Exile of the spirit begins when we believe the world is a big place and we are its tiny prisoners.

201. Our Own Decisions

Those times when a parent stands back as the child decides, watching from afar the consequences yet always there with the child—they are the greatest trial of a parent's love, the ultimate act of parenting.

They are not always possible, often not reasonable, but they are the point at which the child becomes his or her own being.

So, too, when G_d hides His face, that is when He shows His most awesome might, His deepest love.

202. Decisions

At some point, you may need to make a decision as follows:

There is a small, but good thing you could do. But you are afraid that by doing it you may lose out on a much greater and longer-lasting good in the future.

Consider this: We are not prophets. None of us can tell what tomorrow will bring. All we can do is live in the here and now.

Do whatever good comes your way, *when* it comes your way—no matter how small it may seem.

203. UnProphets

If we were prophets or people of vision, we would see what is important and what is not, what will bear fruits and what will remain barren. But we are simple people in an age of confusion. Our lives are filled with uncertainties—anything could happen; we have no way of telling.

We cannot decide which good deed is important and which will bear fruit. Neither are we expected to make our decisions that way.

What's expected of us is to simply grab whatever G_d sends our way, and do our very best at it. What will come of it? What is its purpose? That only He needs to know.

204. Bread From Heaven

Your place is the wilderness. The bread you eat falls
from heaven. The basket in which you collect it is
your attitude.

Clutch your basket tight and your manna will have no
place to rest. Open it up and look to the heavens and
your basket will always be full.

205. Grasping Bread From Heaven

Spirituality is like manna. Bread from heaven is great food, but most people have a need to sink their teeth into some solid stuff of this coarse world. Something they can count and measure and hold on to.

Just like manna, many people are fearful of any subject that borders on the spiritual. It is the unknowableness of it—that you can't grasp it in your hand or tally it up along with your assets—that causes people to shun it, run from it, or even deny it exists.

But they are running from themselves. We are spiritual beings in essence, far more than we are a body with a bank account. Without spiritual nourishment we are plagued by insatiable cravings, like a body lacking essential vitamins.

For the human being, inner peace is only achieved by first surrendering to the unknown.

206. Financial Planning

Advice from the Rebbe's namesake, Rabbi Menachem Mendel of Lubavitch, the "Tzemach Tzedek":

Determine how much you need to provide for your family needs. Then put a bucket just the right size out in the rain—meaning, get into a business that can make that sum of money. Next, pray for compassion.

Know, however, that sometimes all your buckets, as well, are handed to you from above. Sometimes you don't decide how G_d will bless you with an income to support your family. Sometimes you are Joseph, captured and tied to a destiny too great for you to fathom.

Then your job is just to do the best you can with whatever you're given—honestly and earnestly. And put your confidence in your real Employer.

207. Simple Advice

Ask advice from those with experience.

They will provide you cheaply that which they acquired at great expense.

from a letter

208. Angry at the World

Why are you so surprised to find evil and corruption running amok everywhere you look? This world is the coarsest and harshest of all worlds, the ultimate concealment of the Infinite Light. Almost all of it is darkness and emptiness. Only a tiny spark of good is buried deep within to sustain it.

You could spend your lifetime dwelling on the outrages and scandals, the travesties and the ripoffs…

—or your could take a moment to search for that spark. You could find it, grasp it, fan its flame. From within its aura, you will see the darkness shining brighter than the heavens.

In that moment of light, the night will never have been.

209. Finding Perfection

You have to begin with the knowledge that there is

nothing perfect in this world.

Our job is not to hunt down perfection and live within it.

It is to take whatever broken pieces we have found and

sew them together as best we can.

to a girl who
wanted to
leave her
school for
what she
thought to be
a better one.

210. Time is Sacred

The first creation was Time. It began and it will end and then it will be no more.

Each breath, each tick, each beat of the heart comes only once. None will never repeat itself precisely. Every instant of life is a raw but precious stone, beckoning, pleading, "Unleash my potential, unlock my secret, do with me something to reveal my purpose of being! For I am here only this one time, and then never again."

And so that is our primary mission: To elevate Time and to make it holy.

211. Control of Time

When you take control of your life, the first place to start is with Time: Where have your placed the hours of your day?

Soon enough, you will realize you cannot control Time until you first take control of your inner self:

Where have you placed your heart, your mind and your soul? What is important to you? Why have you entered this world?

When your time for study, time for prayer, time for family, time for the world—when all these are anchored with your very being, then all the winds of the world cannot budge them from their proper place. And your soul, as well, remains affixed to its path.

The Word

"And G_d said, 'Let there be light, and there was light.'"
— *Genesis*

"He spoke and it was."
— *Chronicles*

In our view of the world, there is a world and then there are our words we speak about that world. There are objects and we give them names. Things happen and we tell stories about them.

That is our view, the view of the little beings created to inhabit this reality, the view from the inside out. But how does it appear from the outside in, from the perspective of the Creator?

To the Creator, there is nothing here other than His words, nothing other than G_d telling a story to Himself. And inside that grand story are little creatures telling their own smaller stories, creating their own realities within the bubble of a larger reality.

When the first human being began to name the things he saw, the Rebbe explained, he was not simply applying labels—he was completing G_d's work of creation, bringing it into greater focus, creating an identity for each thing that would determine its place in the grand story, attaching those beings to their essence in G_d's primal thought. How can a name affect a live, tangible creature? Because that's all the creature truly is: A word, a name. An articulation of G_d's mind, a crystallization of His thought.

We ourselves are words. We think of ourselves as beings that speak words. But, no, those words are who we are, they extend from our essence and they define our being. They define our place in the world and they define the world in which we are placed.

Every single word.

212. No World

There is no world.

There is no collection of objects following stiff rules. No big machine following a precisely ordered procedure. No concrete, no cement, no steel girders, no materials out of which all is made.

There are no things. There are only events. Ideas happening.

All is but words of a story being told by its author. The music of the Grand Concert Master following His own score. Playing it His own way, living in the nuances, the tiny details of expression. Bending the notes at whim, sometimes changing them altogether, as if to remind the audience, "It's my score, I am the composer. I can do as I wish."

Which just makes it all the more magnificent when He plays by the rules.

There is nothing else but Him.

213.   The Storyteller

Abandon the notion that there is a world and there is a
G_d. It is as fallacious as thinking there is a story and
there is a storyteller.

There is only the storyteller, expressing himself in the
story he tells.

There is only the Unknowable, expressing Himself as
a world.

214. Talking to Himself

He talks with Himself, entertained by His own thoughts.

The thoughts imply a background, which is the world.

But the Torah, those are the thoughts themselves.

215. Defining Your World

We are not passive observers of this universe, but rather partners in its creation. We are the ones who assign each thing its meaning, who bring definition and resolution to an otherwise ambiguous world.

In fact, we are legal witnesses who determine a matter of life or death: For each thing we hold, each event that enters our life, our word declares whether it breathes with G_dly life or simply idles itself into oblivion.

216. Life in Words

Plants live in a world of earth, water, air and sunshine.
Animals live in a world of the body and its senses.
Human beings live within a world of their own words.

The sages called us *the speaking being*, saying our soul
is filled with words. When our words leave us, our very
being goes out within them. We conquer with them. We
declare our mastery over Creation with them. Our
words tell us that we exist.

For us, nothing truly exists until we find a word for it.
All our thoughts of every object and every event are
thoughts of words. Our world is a world not of
sensations and stimuli, but of words.

Build your world with precious words. Fill your days
with words that live and give life.

Memorize words of Torah and of the sages. Have them
ready for any break in your day. Wherever you go,
provide that place an atmosphere of those powerful
words.

217. Focusing Your World

Our advantage as human beings lies in our power to speak, to articulate a nebulous world into meaningful words and phrases. G_d spoke and the world came into being. We speak and bring it into focus.

Our words are the camera that determines reality: According to how we focus, so our world will be. With a small breath of air, we determine whether it is beauty that sprouts from the earth, or monsters growing as large as our imagination.

True, there is a time for all things—even a time to speak in negative terms, to make clear that something is wrong and needs correcting. But there is a caveat to negative words. For if they do not reach their goal, their bitterness still remains.

Speak good words, kind words, words of wisdom, words of encouragement. Like gentle rain upon a dormant field. Eventually, they will coax the seeds beneath the soil to life.

218. The Aura

Each of us builds our own prison or our own palace.

Every conscious thought, every utterance of our lips, every interaction of ours with the world around us leaves its imprint upon an aura that encompasses us and stays with us wherever we go. All life, all blessing, all that is transmitted from Above must pass through that aura. Even the greatest of blessings can be distorted by the aura into ugly noise. Or the aura may resonate with it and amplify it even more.

The rules are simple: An aura of beauty attracts beauty. An aura of love attracts love. An aura of life and joy attracts unbounded light

But rule #1 is even simpler: Only you are the master of that aura. Only you have the permission and the power at any moment to transform your thoughts from the ugly to the beautiful, your words from bitter to sweet, your deeds from death to life.

And so too, your entire world.

219. Wonder Making

If you see someone's faults hanging out and you truly want to help—whether it be a friend, a spouse, your child or even your nemesis—don't say a word about what you have found wrong.

Find something wondrous about that person, perhaps something that nobody ever mentions, and talk about it—to yourself, to those who will listen and sympathize.

In very little time, you will see such a new person, you will believe you are a maker of wonders.

Indeed, we all are.

220. Real Gain

Nothing you have acquired is real unless you worked for it. If you were born a nice guy, the niceness isn't yours. If you started off not so nice, and now you do a little better, that's Divine.

221. Tolerance

As the world came into being, so did tolerance. It may be the most amazing thing about our world—that it can carry on ever so loosely tied, enduring so perfectly in its imperfection.

Without tolerance, the sages say, our world could not stand. Only a world that is allowed to stumble can stand on its own feet. A world of perfection—a world that follows precisely every dictate from Above—is like a fetus that has never left its womb, for it presents nothing of its own. A real world is one whose creatures can pass or fail, can blunder about until they eventually beat their path to the truth.

"And such a world," G_d said, "is worth My tolerance."

222. Reciprocal Tolerance

At every moment, your Creator must decide, "Should I put up once again with this little creature's imperfections and blunders, or is it time to measure things by the scale?"

Then He looks at how you have designed your own universe, the degree and frequency by which you measure those who enter it. And at that same scale, He measures you.

223. Tolerance & Love

There is tolerance that doesn't care. That just looks the other way and goes about its own business. Indifferent tolerance.

Then there is the opposite; the kind of caring that doesn't allow others to step outside the path you believe to be good for them. Suffocating tolerance.

And then there is compassionate tolerance. The kind that recognizes the other person's right to grow, his need to travel along a path and get there on his own—and yet to be there for him nevertheless when he gets lost.

True compassion has room for a thousand private journeys.

Divine Madness

"The prophet is a fool. The man of spirit is mad." (Hosea 9:7)

There is a certain madness to this idea of talking to G_d, of saying "You" to the Ground of Reality — as though this is a person. Like the madness of love or of unbounded joy. Not the madness of a derelict mind, but the madness that rides upon the shoulders of reason, with all its qualities, but beyond. Beyond reason.

Reason scales lofty mountains. Reason alone can pull back the curtains and find G_d there, hiding within existence. "Just as I extend from Mind, says Reason, "so the pulse of life, the path of the electron, the entire cosmic order extends from one magnificent Mind." And what is that Mind? It is *That Which Is*. As the four letter name of G_d, a conjugation of the verb *to be*.

But only madness could imagine entering a conversation with *That Which Is*.

Reason stands on the threshold, trembling to open the door to her own womb, though a blinding light bursts from between the cracks. For in that place, she knows, there is no reason. She has shown the way, but now she must step aside for madness to break in.

Madness kicks down the door and liberates G_d. Madness, the insanity of joy and of love, knows no fetters, respects no bounds. Madness says, "Why should I limit you to that which is? You can be found wherever You wish to be found! You can care about whatever You wish to care! Without reason—for You Yourself have no beginning, no reason to dictate to You how things must be."

And so this madness, this wild, radical sense of freedom that breathes within the human spirit and lifts him from object to person, this madness finds its partner in G_d. "Both of us are free," this madness says. "My freedom comes from You and Your freedom becomes real in me. So let us be partners and I will speak to the Ground of Reality and say *You.*"

chabad.org/427397

224. Greatness Unlimited

To some, G_d is great because He makes the wind blow. For others, because He projects space and time, matter and energy out of the void. The men of thought laugh and say He is far beyond any of this, for His Oneness transcends all things and remains unaltered even by the event of Creation.

We Jews, this is what we have always said:

G_d is so great, He stoops to listen to the prayer of a small child; He paints the petals of each wildflower and awaits us there to catch Him doing so; He plays with the rules of the world He has made to comfort the oppressed and support those who champion justice and goodness. He transcends the bounds of higher and lower. He transcends all bounds.

225. G_d Within

Before the Baal Shem Tov, people thought of G_d as the One who directs all things from above. The Baal Shem Tov taught that the vital force of each thing, the place from which comes its personality, its sense of pain and pleasure, its growth and life—that itself is G_d.

Not that this is all of G_d. It is less than a glimmer of G_d. G_d is entirely beyond all descriptions.

But that life force is G_d. G_d as He is found within each creature He has made.

226. Signature

He inscribed His signature within each thing He made. On the outside each thing is finite, but on the inside you will find the signature of infinitude.

Open anything you like, examine it carefully and you will see. A puddle of water, a grain of sand, a splotch of mud on the wall. There is nothing that does not contain endless wonders. Nothing that could not involve a lifetime study.

Because all of them He made with His infinite wisdom.

227. Heresy

I agree with the heretics. The god the world believes in does not exist

—a god who peers in through the clouds at a world he sometime made and plays with it as a child plays in the sand...

Such a god is no more than another of Man's toys. A man has a house, he has a car, a job, a wife and children. So he must also have a god. And he creates one in his image.

Live in a mythical world, you will have a mythical god.

The real G-d is not a figment of the human mind. We are an artifact of His.

228. Getting Real

Why is G-d not real to you?

Because your god is not real.

You begin with, "Here I am, standing in this world," and then you append, "and G-d is watching down on me."

If you begin with the premise of your own reality, how will you end up with a real G-d?

G-d is watching down on you—and you and your world are a glimmer of His presence.

229. Grasping Change

That which can be grasped will change.

That which does not change cannot be grasped.

230. Raw Truth

Truth is simple. It has no clothes, no boundaries to
define it. But we cannot grasp the immaculately simple.
We cannot perceive truth without clothing.

So Truth dresses up for us, in the stories of the Torah,
in its sage advice, in its blueprint of the cosmos. And
then, before we can imagine that we have grasped
Truth, it switches its clothes. It tells us another
story—one irreconcilable with the first; new
advice—different, contradictory; another model of
how things are—in which each thing has changed
its place.

The fool is confused, he says, "Truth has lied!"

The wise person sees within and finds a simple,
unbounded light.

231. Being & Not Being

He made His world of contradictions, opposites that combine as one. At their nexus, a world is formed: Neither can exist without the other, all function together as a single whole.

Being and not being, infinity and finitude, light and darkness, form and matter, quantity and quality, totality and detail, community and individual, giving and withholding.

They are mere modalities—He Himself is none of them. He mixes them and matches them at whim.

Paradox is our window to beyond.

232. Two Paths

If you find yourself on a single path to truth—

through prayer and meditation,

through acts of kindness and love,

through any other path of a singular modality and tone

—you are on the wrong path.

There is no one path to truth.

Truth is not at the end of a path.

Truth is found in the journey of two opposite paths

at once.

233. Real Motives

No person can know his own inner motives.

He may be kind because kindness brings him pleasure.

He may be wise because wisdom is music to his soul.

He may become a martyr burned in fire because his
nature is to defy, his nature is to be fire.

When can you know that your motives are sincere?
Only when it is not within your nature to do this thing.

And how do you know that it is not within your nature?
Only when you travel two opposite paths at once.

234. Being Paradox

Be simple. In whatever you do, in whatever form you take, in whatever you decide you are, retain memory that you are not that.

When the Red Sea split, the water stood as a wall to the right and the water stood as a wall to the left. How did the wind do that? Because the wind was beyond nature, beyond right and left. Beyond direction.

Be as that wind—beyond nature. Never travel a single road. Always walk through the splitting of the Red Sea.

235. Both Ways

One who loves must learn fear. One who fears must learn love. The thinker must do. The doer must think. The pacifist must fight, the fighter must find peace.

If you flow as a river, burn as a fire. If you burn as a furnace, flow as a river. If you fly as a bird, sit firm as a rock. If you sit firmly, then fly as a bird.

Be a fire that flows. A rock that flies. Love with fear and fear with love.

For we are not fire, not water, not air, not rocks, not thoughts, not deeds, not fear, not love.

We are G_dly beings.

236. G_d's Question

Before He brought forth the cosmos out of
nothingness, it was no more than a game He played in
His own mind, pondering,

"Should it be? Or should it not?"

Then He created all things according to the tension of
that thought, and out of all things of that creation He
formed Adam. Within Adam He breathed this breath of
life, containing this Divine struggle, and Adam became a
living being.

So Adam awoke and he began to ponder, "Do I exist?
Or do I not? Should there be a world? Or should there
not? Why should there be anything at all?"

And now it is up to us.

237. Finishing Touches

When the Infinite Creator created the finite world, He left over an essential task for Adam to complete: To reveal the unity of finite and infinite.

But how is Adam capable of completing G_d's work?

Because Adam is that place within G_d where the finite and the infinite meet.

238. Who's First?

If we had been here first and then set the criteria for a very perfect G_d, certainly one of our requirements would be that He be logical and understandable.

Too bad for us—He was here first.

As for logic, that came later.

239. Impossible

He could have made a world that would look at itself and explain itself according to its own rules.

But He made a world with such rules, that according to its own rules it cannot exist.

He wanted a world with wonder.

240. Beauty and Beauty

There are two kinds of beautiful thoughts:

There are ideas that are beautiful because
we understand.

And there are ideas that are beautiful although we do
not understand. All we grasp of them is their beauty.

This itself is something beautiful: That an idea can
reach down and touch a mind that cannot grasp it.

Perhaps here we are even closer to the essential
wisdom—for what is wisdom and understanding in
essence, other than beauty and delight unfolding in
our minds?

241. Why the Heavens?

Why were we made so small, with such great heavens

above our heads?

Because He desired creatures that would

know wonder.

see Bosi
L'Gani
5752

242. Essential Good

At the core of all our thoughts and beliefs lies the

conviction that the underlying reality is wholly good.

That evil lies only at the surface, a thin film of distortion

soon to be washed away by the waves.

243. A Real Fool

To live with the Infinite, you must allow yourself to be a fool at times. To be a simpleton who does good earnestly, ignorant and oblivious to everyone else's opinion.

If you stop to ponder, debate and refute them, they will catch you in their snare. You already know what is right—just do it like a simple, complete idiot.

Learn from this world we live in: The world is a fool— only that it is a mindless, stupid fool. You be a fool who reaches beyond the mind.

244. Fear of Joy

People are afraid of joy. They are afraid they'll get out
of hand and lose control.

These people haven't experienced real joy—the joy
that comes from doing something G_dly and beautiful
with all your heart. The fact is, there is nothing that will
lift you higher.

Where there is that joy, the Divine Presence can enter.
Where there is that joy, there are no pits to fall into,
and all obstacles evaporate into thin air.

Failure & Return

In truth, there is a certain nobleness to sin, something essential to our humanness that makes us more precious than the angels. As soon as any transactional relationship is set in place—as in, "You do this, I will do that. If you don't do this, then…"— our impulse is to break free. We are humans, there is a person inside, we want to relate as people. Not as what we do, but as who we are.

So it is with our spouse, with our children, with friends. We are always testing each other, testing to see just how deep this relationship extends. Testing to see: Are you interested in me, as I know myself? Or are you interested in what you can get from me?

So, too, when it is a relationship with the Inner Mind of the Cosmos. We want to relate to Him from our inner being, from our humanness, not just from our behavior.

Such was the test we put Him to when we built a golden calf. With that rebellion, we asked, "Even if we break these rules You gave us, do You still love us then?"

Such was the test of Eve. With the story of Eve ends the story of G_d's creation—His top-down management scheme—and begins the story of humanity. The story for which He created the universe to begin with. The story of real, live people who might do what you want, but might end up doing just about anything. And whose lives are valuable for that alone.

If so, if sin is so beautiful, perhaps we should continue to sin?

No, because in the dark shadow of sin itself there is no beauty, only in its resolution.

This is what was missing in Eve's story: the resolution. In all the instances where her story reoccurs—with her firstborn son, Cain; with the making of the golden calf; with David and Bathsheba; with the destruction of the Temple—in all those sins and betrayals, the story continues and resolves. There is remorse, return and a deepening of the relationship. The contractual agreement is renewed—but now with a deeper foundation, an intimate one based on the inner person and an Inner G_d.

But Eve's sin, the first disconnect from which all other fissures stem, remains unresolved. She, the mother of us all, bequeathed us this job, to heal the wound that she forged, the schism between body and spirit, woman and man, humankind and G_d. And so, to create that inner relationship with the Divine, that relationship which Eve was desperately seeking.

chabad.org/131166

245. Dance With the Other

As a mother with the baby she holds in her arms, as a father with his child, as two in courtship or in marriage, so we are with Him. One chases, the other runs away. One runs away, the other chases. One initiates, the other responds. The other initiates, the one responds. It is a dance, a game, a duet that plays as surely as the pulse of life.

Until one falls away and becomes estranged. Then the other looks and says, "This is not an other. We are one and the same." And so, they return to each other's arms once again.

It is a great mystery, but in estrangement, there is found the deepest bond[TF48].

246. Self-Pity

Self-pity is nothing less than an impulse to destroy your own self. And this is its script:

"This is the way you were made. These are the facts of your situation. It's bad. Worse than anybody else in the whole world. In fact, it's so bad, it's impossible to do anything about it. And therefore, you are free from any responsibility to clean it up. Nobody can blame you for anything."

Self-pity is a liar and a thief. A liar, because everyone is granted the power to clean up his own mess, if only he will try. A thief, because it steals away every opportunity you have to move on in life.

247. Time Machine

If you could travel back in time, what could you change? The world, its past and its present all belong to the Creator. All is as He wills it to be.

Perhaps you could replay some crucial scenes and distance yourself from the mess that occurred. Perhaps you could jump in and grab credit for some of the good.

But for that, you don't need a time machine. All you need is to stand right where you are and say, "I messed up. I lost my chance. I learned my lesson and now I will do things differently."

You will change yourself. You will change your past. You will say, "I am no longer the person who lived in that past."

In fact, you *do* have a time machine.

248. Waiting for Fruition

If the world did not need you and you did not need this world, you would never have come here. G_d does not cast His precious child into the pain of this journey without purpose.

You say you cannot see a reason. Why should it surprise you that a creature cannot fathom the plan of its Creator?

Move on; plant seeds with faith. Eventually the fruits of your labor will blossom for all to see.

249. Wheat and Dates

Some grow as wheat of the field, in a single season breaking through the ground and ripening. But their produce must be shelled and ground and refined and kneaded and baked before providing good to the world—and much must be cast aside.

Others grow as the date palm, which may weather seventy years before its first fruit arrives. But it is fruit that is sweet and satisfying to the one that picks it, and every part of the palm and its fruit have something of value to provide.

to a teacher
who was
anxious to
see in her
students the
fruits of her
labor.

250. Flight

When Man desired to fly, two paths lay before him: To create vehicles lighter than air, or to use the air's resistance to his advantage. In the end, the second path proved more successful.

It turns out that when you wish to fly above, resistance is to your advantage. In fact, it carries you higher than the angels.

251. The Highest High

What could be higher than having found truth on
your own?

All worlds were made, all barriers put in place, every veil
over G_dliness hung, and the soul plummeted from its
pristine height into the confusion of this harsh world—

—all for this one thing alone: That you should uncover
truth on your own.

252. Darkness With Hope

There are dark jewels in this world that can be salvaged, purified and taken as precious bounty for the good.

And there is darkness itself, the essential absence of light, that must only wait its time to expire.

How can we tell between them?

If the darkness allows your light in without resistance, it is simply waiting for it to be extinguished. For this darkness, there is no hope.

If the darkness fights back, it is telling you there is something there worth fighting for. For this darkness, there is hope.

253. Your Beast

We all have our animal inside. The point is not simply to muzzle that animal, but to harness its power. To determine what sort of an animal this is and what can be done with it.

A sheep, for example, is easily domesticated and doesn't care to hurt anyone, while an ox may kick and gore. But did you ever see a sheep plow a field?

254. Out From Under the Blanket

Anxieties, worries, feelings of inadequacy and failure—all these smother and cripple the soul from doing its job. You need to find the appropriate time to deal with them. But don't carry them around the whole day.

During the day, you are Adam or Eve before they tasted the fruit of good and evil.

255. The Fair Maiden's Hero

"He found her in the field. The maiden cried out, but there was no one to hear."—Deuteronomy 22:23

Rabbi Menachem Mendel of Lubavitch explained:

Captured by Esau, a brute of the field, raped and abused, the G_dly soul within us screams spontaneously from its depths.
And no one hears.

No one. Nothingness. The nothingness from which everything begins. Not a being, not just the Source of All Being, but the core-essence of G_d, beyond all being. There, her cry is heard.

Nothingness hears. Just as the screams of a fair maiden will awaken the hidden power of her beloved to overcome mighty armies and slay awesome giants; so too, the cries of the soul from her captivity—the core of her being reaches to the core of the Infinite Above.

Anything could change. Even the past.

256. Progressive Failure

There are two ways to ascend: You can step upward, leaving one foot in its place as the other moves ahead. Or you can crouch down and leap.

This is the true meaning of failure: Failure is not just a setback. Everything in life is a step forward, because everything has meaning.

So too, failure: It is the crouch before the jump, the break away from the past so that we can leap into the future.

257. Kosher Yearnings

A man sits and yearns for a thing he should not have. The yearning in itself is good—a man who does not yearn does not live. To live is to yearn. But the form this yearning has taken is death itself.

So the form must be crushed. Extinguished like the embers of an abandoned campfire in a dry forest. Once that is done, the inner yearning can be freed, the flame of life that burns inside. That was always good. The yearning that is life.

258. Bouncing Up

Why does Man destroy? Why does he wreak havoc in
the world?

This world was designed so that there is no progress
forward without first a step backward. Night comes
before day, pain before pleasure, confusion
before wisdom.

But then G_d made man, who strives beyond the design
of things, who yearns to leap past nature, to embrace
the infinite.

Man, too, must first fall so that he can leap upward.
But since his leap is beyond nature, he must first fall
beneath it.

That is sin—a fall beneath nature.

And that is the power of return

—to leap beyond nature.

259. Delights

G_d has many delights:

The delight that comes from a pure and simple act of love.

Greater than that, the delight that comes from an act of beauty sparkling in the darkness.

Greater than that, the delight when a child who has run away returns with all her heart.

All the world was formed from G_d's delight. There is nothing else.

260. Higher Pain

The root of illness is the yearning of all life to return home. For the Mother of All Life has descended from Her place on high to give life and to that place She longs to return. And with that longing She gives life.

If so, at the core of life's pleasure lies pain, an ache that says, "This is not my true place, I must be higher, somewhere beyond me. But I am not there."

From that anguish comes not only life, but also illness into our world—from our futile efforts to alleviate the pain with artificial sweeteners, with habits that pretend to fill that void with vanities that are not life at all.

To live is to yearn, but not to be a fool.

261. Our Voice

What do we bring to the table?

Our brains, our power, our art are all from Him.

Even when we decide with our own free will to do good and to restrain ourselves from the opposite, we are only playing our part in a cosmic script for which we were formed.

But when we mess up, we can call the Infinite Light, "Father," and ask forgiveness.

That is not in the script. That is from beyond.

Way beyond.

262. Father's Anticipation

Delight lies at the core of heart and mind.

Deep within a father's soul, even the father whose face
is stern and heart is cold, yet, without doubt, deep
within lies the spark of the child he has born, his
innermost delight.

Within the child lies that spark as well. Perhaps even
more dormant, quiet—not even a flicker—yet there.

When one spark awakens, the other flames in
resonance.

When the Master of All Things sits in judgment over His
world, He awaits the moment His children will call Him
'Father.' Then the spark below awakens the spark
above, the innermost delight.

263. Father as Tutor

Imagine a father tutoring his child, as any tutor will teach a student.

Imagine the child does well, and the father returns a smile of approval, as any good tutor would do.

But then, the father can no longer restrict himself to his role as tutor. He laughs, he slaps his child affectionately on the back, they both laugh together, not as a teacher and student, but as only a father and child could do, the father saying in his laugh, "I always had this pride, this delight in you, that you are my child. I only needed this excuse to show it."

Above, our Father awaits His chance to laugh with us.

Legacy

Some think of people much as we think of cars on a highway: Each with its own origin and destination, relating to one another only to negotiate lane changes and left-hand turns. For cars, closeness is danger, loneliness is freedom.

People are not cars. Cars are dead. People live. Living beings need each other, nurture one another, share destinies and reach them together. When you're alive, closeness is warmth, loneliness is suffocating.

People belong to families. Families make up communities. Communities make up the many colorful peoples of the world. And all those peoples make up a single, magnificent body with a single soul called humankind.

Some chop this body into six or seven billion fragments and roll it back into a single mush. They want each person to do his or her own thing and relate equally to every other individual on the planet. They don't see the point of distinct peoples. They feel such distinctions just get in the way.

But we are not mush. We are leaves extending from twigs branching out from larger twigs on branches of larger branches until we reach the trunk and roots of us all. Each of us has our place on this tree of life, each our source of nurture—and on this tacit agreement the tree relies for its very survival.

None of us walks alone. Each carries the experiences of ancestors wherever he or she roams, along with their troubles, their traumas, their victories, their hopes and their aspirations. Our thoughts grow out from their thoughts, our destiny is shaped by their goals. At the highest peak we ever get to, there they are, holding our hand, pushing us upward, providing the shoulders on which we stand. And we share those shoulders, that consciousness, that heritage with all the brothers and sisters of our people.

That's why your own people are so important: If you want to find peace with any other person in the world, you've got to start with your own brothers and sisters. Until then, you haven't yet found peace within your own self. And only when you've found peace within your self can you help us find peace for the entire world.

Take my people—the Jewish people. Every one of us is a brother or sister of a great family of many thousands of years. Where one of us walks, there walk sages and martyrs, heroes and heroines, legends and miracles, all the way back to Abraham and Sarah, the first two Jews who challenged the whole world with their ideals. There walk the tears, the blood and the chutzpah of millennia, the legacy of those who lived, yearned and died for a World To Come, a world the way it was meant to be.

Should I abandon them to join a homogenous mush? No one would benefit. For their destiny is my destiny. In them I am fulfilled, in each and every one of them and all of us together. And upon their oneness relies the oneness of the entire world.

Because my people is a vital organ of a single, magnificent body that breathes with a single set of lungs, pulsates with a single heart, draws from a single well of consciousness. As are the people of the Squamish Nation. And the Inuit. And the Swahili. And the Turks and the Persians and all of us.

If we try to do each other's job, we're in a big mess. When we find our place in that grand whole and do all we can from there, then the world is healthy.

chabad.org/142444

264. Life's Roots

We are trees, living two lives at once. One life breaking through the soil into this world. Where, with all our might, we struggle to rise above it, grapple for its sun and its dew, desperate not to be torn away by the fury of its storms or consumed by its fires.

Then there are our roots, deep under the ground, unmoving and serene. They are our ancient mothers and fathers, who lie within us at our very core. For them, there is no storm, no struggle. There is only the One, the Infinite, for Whom all the cosmos with all its challenges are nothing more than a fantasy renewed every moment from the void.

Our strength is from our bond with them. With their nurture we will conquer the storm and bring beauty to the world we were planted within.

265. Diamonds and Emeralds

One man carries rocks for a livelihood. Give him

emeralds and all he sees is more rocks.

Another carries diamonds with devotion and care.

Give him the emeralds and he exclaims, "What beauty

is here!"

He who values his own heritage is best able to

appreciate the beauty that others hold.

from a letter
to Rabbi Jonathan
Sacks in his early
years

266. Youthful Wisdom

Wisdom lives in the future, and from there it speaks to us. There is no such thing as wisdom of the past.

Wisdom preceded the world and wisdom is its destiny. With each passing moment, wisdom becomes younger as we come closer to the time when it is born and breathes the air of day.

Our ancient mothers and fathers, the sages, all those from whom we learn wisdom—they are not guardians of the past. They are messengers of the future.

The truth can never be
old-fashioned.
It was never in fashion
to begin with.

267. Inner Engravings

The soul is full of words, some inscribed,
some engraved.

The words inscribed are not of the essence—they
come to the soul from the outside, from life and its
experiences. Therefore, they may fade and fall away,
perhaps to be replaced by other words.

The words engraved are of the soul itself—just as
engravings are no more than the form of the stone.
When the soul finds quietude, those words are there. If
the soul is in turmoil, or soiled by experience, those
engravings need only be cleaned and uncovered. But
they can never be torn away.

Those same words that compose the fabric of the soul,
they are also engraved in a holy fire within the depths
of the Soul of All Things. They are the words that
Moses heard and inscribed on stone and on
parchment. And at times, when you immerse yourself in
the Torah and the words of its sages, when you allow
them entry to touch your soul, you may hear those
words resonating inside.

268. Conviction

All the elaborate proofs and deep philosophy will never stand you firmly on your feet. The only thing that will make it work for you is your own inherent conviction.

Because even at the time your mind is not thinking about whether this is true or not, you yourself know within that it is so, and know that you believe it to be so. It is a conviction all the winds of the world cannot uproot, for it comes from within and from the heritage of your ancestors who believed as well.

The challenge is only to ignore those doubts that come to you from the outside, and to allow that inner knowledge to shine through and guide you.

from a letter to
a woman who
suffered chronic
uncertainty.

269. To Each His Path

Just as it is a mitzvah to direct someone on to the path where he belongs, so too it is a crime to direct someone onto a path that does not belong to him. Each person is born with a path particular to his or her soul, generally according to the culture into which he or she was born.

There are universal truths, the inheritance of all of us since Adam and Noah. In them we are all united.

But we are not meant to all be the same. Our differences are as valuable to our Creator as our similarities.

270. Differences

Don't be afraid of the other person because he is different from you. There is far more in common between any two human beings than there are differences.

As for the differences, think of them as the hooks that hold us together. Differences are the thing we have most in common.

The Rebbe was talking to children and discussing relationships between Jews and non-Jews.

271. The Field of Your Mind

A creative mind is a fertile field. But that may simply mean that the weeds are taller and grow faster.

First, soften your mind's soil, plough its furrows. Open it to the wisdom that rains down from the heavens; let the dew of Torah sink into your soul, the seeds laid by tzaddikim enter your heart. Learn to lie still as they awaken and take root. Quietly await the spring.

In the place of thorns and a tangle of weeds will grow a bountiful garden. Where once wild and brazen delusions sprang forth, a tightly focussed beam of light will shine.

272. The Atheist

The atheist, too, has a god, and it is himself.

The idolater at least understands there is something greater than him, something beyond the grasp of his physical senses, some external forces to which he is subject.

But for the atheist, all the universe is defined by his own understanding, all ethics are subject to his approval and even he himself is an artifact of his own mind. He is a self-made man, for he creates his own universe and squeezes himself inside it.

273. Truth Anywhere

Truth can come from anywhere—there is nothing that does not have its truth. Because, without a spark of truth, nothing can exist. Not even falseness.

Therefore, the wise man is he who knows how to learn truth from every person and discover the truth of each thing.

274. Live Study

There are two types of study: The study of a static object, something of the past, something long dead. All that's needed for this study is cold, hard intellect.

Then there is the study of a vibrant, living being. To know it, you must live with it, be humbled before it, feel its life and spirit.

Truth is the ultimate living Being.

275. Forbidden Water

Sometimes the sages tell us, "This wisdom is out of bounds. This contains truth for which you are not yet ready."

If your soul is intact, the thirst for that wisdom will become unbearable and you will have no choice but to satisfy it. In truth, that is the inner reason we are told such things.

276. Convergence Point

There is no such thing as a mitzvah done alone. In a mitzvah, space, time and consciousness converge. You nod your consent, and a flood of generations flows through you to do the rest. Together with you, every soul of our people, wherever they may be, are swept along in the current.

277. Multifaceted Being

Each of us has deficiencies, but as a whole we
are complete.

Each one is perfected by his fellow, until we make a
perfect whole.

278. Dancing With Them

This self we are conscious of, it is only a tiny portion of the whole, a finely focussed constriction of a beam, the tip of a peninsula from a great continent of light.

Upstream lies unimaginable wealth, storehouses of treasures left by many generations. There can be found very G_dly act done by our holy mothers and fathers, all the strength and courage of every martyr, the unlimited power of G_d's breath within us.

Next time you dance and sing in the joy of a beautiful deed, hear your holy mothers and fathers of ages past dancing and singing along.

279. Our Land

The nations cannot understand why the Jewish people should have a land. "If it is G–d and scriptures and heaven that you are all about," they claim, "then why do you want a piece of earth? Is G–d in a place? Will you find G–d in settling land, in governing a country, in defending it? Make up your mind: Is it heaven you want, or earth?"

Those words, perhaps, are never said. They are quiet words, engraved within the human psyche. And they are the bias behind all their contentions with us: We don't belong here, on earth, where they belong, playing by their rules. Because G–d is in the heavens, and the earth belongs to humankind.

But this is the mission of the Jewish people: For all to see that the same G–d in heaven is here within the earth, within all the endeavors of humankind. For there is nothing else but Him.

Beginning with that specific, well-defined, very special piece of earth to which our destiny is tied.

280. Bringing Closer

"My job is not to distance anyone, but to draw them closer. If there is a person who needs to be pushed away, let that be someone else's job."

from a
letter of
the Rebbe

281. Moses Inside

In each of us glows a spark of Moses. He is our teacher. A teacher's job is to open a small window for the inner knowledge to pour down into the conscious mind.

How do you awaken Moses? By waking yourself.

How do you awaken yourself? By connecting to someone in whom Moses is awake.

Only the awakened can waken others.

AfterWord

Eventually everybody asks, "What now after the Rebbe has passed on?"

First of all, you must know—even though it doesn't answer our question—that the Rebbe is still here with us. Just as a parent who leaves this world is still with his or her children—but much, much more so. Just as a teacher who leaves the classroom to see how well she has taught her pupils to learn on their own—she is even more present in her absence. Just as any tzadik, for whom death is no more than a passing from the confines of the body to a freedom to work within this world without such limitations. But even more so.

For a tzadik as transcendent as the Rebbe, none of the events of this world, not even death, effect any real change. His life is truth, and truth is constant. He guides those who are bound to him as he guided them before, and continues to channel light and blessing into our world and for those in need, as he always has.

The only change is for us, that the rods and cones in the back of our retina cannot see a tzadik before them. And that is our question: How can we be expected to carry on with our window shades down?

The question is really a larger one: Where are all the tzadikim when we need them most? Once upon a time, people lived a simple life and had clear direction from their teachers and parents. They believed with simple faith that wonders and miracles could happen, and that G_d could speak with Man. What need did they have for tzadikim? Now, with our disillusionment, confusion and apathy, *now* we need someone above all this to show us that G_d is still possible. Yet now, more than ever, we are alone.

What use is a closed window? What does it provide? Is the whole point only that we should experience the pain of withdrawal? To yearn for the sunlight which we once had?

So here the metaphor breaks down. Because the job of a tzadik is not simply to bring in light from some place outside. Light that lasts only as long as the window is open is not the true light. The true light is everywhere, within everything, and the tzadik comes to reveal it there as well.

This is the lesson the teacher can only accomplish through his absence. As long as the teacher is present, the student has no need to look inside to find truth. Neither has he truly absorbed any of it. There is the student and there is the knowledge shown to him and as much as the student may bask in that light—even though it be the light of his own soul—they remain foreigners to one another.

Now the teacher hides, the window is closed and the student cries out that he cannot see. That crying, that yearning, that itself is the first glimmer of the student's own light shining from within.

This is what the Rebbe himself told us shortly before his stroke and handed to us in writing: He wrote that the job of a rebbe is to put people in touch with the light that is their own essence and being. But the job of absorbing that light and making it real, this can only be accomplished by the people themselves.

"When they cry out 'How long will this spiritual exile be?' it is only because I have told them to. What can I do so that they will cry out sincerely from within? The only thing I can do is to hand the matter over to each one of you."

The tzadik has shown us where to look. Now he hides so we may discover.

Soak in the wisdom of the Rebbe, not as words, not as ideas, but striving to feel the tzadik within them. Find a place where the teacher and student merge.

Once enough of us have done this, it will be time for the blind to be pulled from over our eyes, for all the walls to be dissolved and we will see the world for what it truly is. We will know wisdom once again from the Rebbe's mouth—until there will no longer be a teacher and a student. We will have arrived.

May that be sooner than we can imagine.

About the Rebbe

Rabbi Menachem Mendel Schneerson inherited the line of chassidic masters that began with the Baal Shem Tov and carried it into the modern day. He studied Talmud and Kabbalah from his father, and later from his father-in-law, the previous rebbe of Lubavitch. He received rabbinical ordination from the Gaon of Rogatchov, Rabbi Yosef Rosen, as an adolescent.

He also studied the sciences at the University of Berlin from the years 1928–1932, when Albert Einstein and Erwin Schrodinger were faculty members, and then the humanities at the Sorbonne from 1934–1938. In 1941, he escaped occupied France. Upon arrival in America, he was enlisted as an engineer on classified military projects.

With the passing of his father-in-law, Rabbi Yosef Yitzchaak Schneerson, in 1950, after an entire year of petitions and pressure, he accepted the mantle of leadership of the Lubavitch Chassidim.

Immediately he began sending agents to assist Jewish communities worldwide. In the sixties, he embraced the spirit of nonconformity, which he saw as a spiritual reawakening. Through his work, tens of thousands of Jews returned to their roots and their spiritual heritage, as thousands of institutions were established in every part of the globe.

Every day, bags of mail arrived at his door, with requests for advice and guidance. He read each one personally and much of this book is based on his responses. However, his frequent informal public talks—or 'farbrengens'—are the major source. These have been edited and published in over forty volumes.

In the eighties, he told his students they must also be concerned with the spiritual welfare of non-Jews, encouraging all people to follow the instructions given to Noah and his descendants. He pushed for spirituality and ethics to be introduced into the public school system, stating that this was the only way to establish a stable society.

In recognition of these efforts, in 1983, U.S. Congress proclaimed the Rebbe's birthday 'Education Day USA' and awarded him the National Scroll of Honor.

Throughout his life, he was driven by a vision of the Messianic Era, and this came to a fore in his later years. He saw the advances of science, of communications technology, the events of glasnost and other events as signs of a new era dawning. He repeatedly told his students that their entire goal must be to prepare the world for these imminent times.

In 1995, the Rebbe became the first to receive posthumously the Congressional Gold Medal, an award granted to only 130 Americans since Thomas Jefferson, for 'outstanding and lasting contributions.'

His students consider him to remain their teacher and leader of the Lubavitcher Chassidim, even after his passing in 1994. Men of spirit such as this live forever, in this world as well.

About the Compiler

Tzvi Freeman was born in Vancouver, Canada, where he became involved at an early age in Yoga, Tao and radical politics. In 1975, he left a career as a classical guitarist and composer to study Talmud and Jewish mysticism for nine years. Since then, he has balanced a career of freelance writing and multimedia software design. He has written feature articles for Game Developer Magazine and was appointed to the educational advisory board of Vivendi Interactive.

He now writes regularly for Chabad.org and has been a featured speaker in North America and Europe.

Rabbi Freeman currently resides in Thornhill, Ontario, with his wife, Nomi, and their children.